Conflicts in Urban Education

Conflicts in Urban Education

edited by

S H E L D O N   M A R C U S *and*

H A R R Y   N.   R I V L I N

BASIC BOOKS, INC., Publishers

New York / London

The Authors

DOYLE BORTNER is Dean of the School of Education at The City
College of New York. He was formerly a faculty member at
Jersey City State College, Bates College and Temple Univer-
sity. His publications include *Public Relations for Teachers*.

ROBERT A. DENTLER is Director for the Center for Urban Educa-
tion. He previously taught at Columbia University, Cornell
University, Wesleyan University, Dartmouth College, and the
University of Kansas. His publications include *The Urban
R's, Race Relations as the Problem in Urban Education, Big
City Dropouts and Illiterates*.

FRED M. HECHLINGER is a member of the editorial board of the
New York Times and the former Education Editor. He is the
recipient of numerous journalistic awards for outstanding writing. His publications include *The Big Red Schoolhouse, Teen-
Age Tyranny, Pre-School Education, An Adventure in Education: Connecticut Leads the Way*.

WILLIAM C. KVARACEUS is Chairman of the Department of Education at Clark University. Formerly, he was a faculty member
at Harvard University, Tufts University, Boston University
and the Director of the Juvenile Delinquency of the National

Education Association. His publications include *The Community and the Delinquent, Juvenile Delinquency and the School, If Your Child is Handicapped.*

SHELDON MARCUS is the Director of Fordham University's Urban Institute and a faculty member in the School of Education. He was previously a faculty member at The City University of New York. Dr. Marcus is the author of numerous publications and has served in the New York City Schools as a teacher and administrator.

JOSEPH MONSERRAT is a member of the New York City Board of Education. He has served as Director of the Migration Division of Department of Labor of the Commonwealth of Puerto Rico and is a member of the New York State Advisory Committee to the United States Civil Rights Commission. Mr. Monserrat was born in Puerto Rico, but raised in New York City and educated in the city's public schools.

REVEREND C. HERBERT OLIVER was Chairman of the Ocean Hill-Brownsville Governing Board and pastor of the Westminster-Bethany United Presbyterian Church. He has served as minister in Northern Maine and Birmingham, Alabama. He is also the former Executive-Secretary of the Inter-Citizens Committee which documents and circulates cases of alleged police brutality.

HARRY N. RIVLIN is presently Dean of the School of Education at Fordham University and Director of the Leadership Training Institute (TTT), sponsored by the United States Office of Education, Department of Health, Education and Welfare. He has also held the position of Dean of Teacher Education at The City University of New York from 1962 to 1966. His publications include *Teaching Adolescents in Secondary School* and *The First Years in College.*

ALBERT SHANKER is President of the United Federation of Teachers and Vice-President of the American Federation of Teachers. He is also a member of the Executive Board of the New York City Central Labor Council, the Board of Directors of the League for Industrial Democracy, and the A. Philip Randolph Institute Board of Trustees of the Center for Urban Education.

ELLIOTT SHAPIRO is an Assistant Superintendent of Schools in the New York City school system. He has taught at Columbia University, The City College of New York and the University of California at Berkeley. Dr. Shapiro is the biographical subject of Nat Hentoff's book, *Our Children Are Dying*.

PHILIP D. VAIRO is Dean of Professional Studies at the University of Tennessee at Chattanooga. From 1967 to 1969 he was Chairman of the division of Curriculum and Teaching at Fordham University. His publications include *How to Teach Disadvantaged Youth* and *Urban Education: Problems and Prospects*.

DOXEY A. WILKERSON is Chairman of the Department of Curriculum and Instruction at Ferkauf Graduate School of Humanities and Social Sciences, Yeshiva University. He is a former faculty member of Howard University, Virginia State College, Jefferson School of Social Science, and Bishop College. His publications include *Compensatory Education for the Disadvantaged*.

Preface

These days *urban* seems to be only half a word, for we seldom hear it used without its being followed immediately by another word, as in *urban problems* or *urban crisis*. It is true, depressingly so, that urban education is facing serious problems. However it is also true that this situation offers education a tremendous opportunity to help solve urban problems, and that urban education has the assets with which to do it. As Hechinger writes in Chapter 1, "Education 1980," ". . . the urban schools in 1980 will either be accomplices to urban disaster or partners in an urban renaissance. Which it will be will be determined by the actions we take, not ten years from now, but this year and next." [p. 18]

Probably the most important asset that urban education has is the people who are leading the kind of actions Hechinger urges. This book brings together the contributions of twelve such leaders, each of whom is playing a vital role in helping to reshape urban schools.

"Conflicts in Education" was chosen as the theme for this book because urban education today is full of conflicts. Conflicts are neither good nor bad per se. Much depends upon what happens as a result of them. Conflicts characterized by emotional scenes, with each side hardening its stand and refusing to hear what the other side is saying, lead only to further and even less productive conflicts. On the other hand, conflicts may lead to clarification of the issues and to the development of new proposals for solutions. Those seeking to solve the problems and to take advantage of the opportunities of urban schools cannot flee from the problems or ignore the conflicts. If conflicts are to lead to progress instead of to confrontations, we must learn to hear, to listen to, and to understand what is being said, even by those with whom we disagree.

This book is an outgrowth of a summer institute conducted by Fordham University's School of Education at Lincoln Center in 1969. Situated in the heart of the nation's greatest city, it is only natural that Fordham should focus its resources and programs on urban education. Its very location suggests both the assets and trials of city schools today. Within a few minutes walk is the Lincoln Center of Performing Arts, with the opera, the theatre, the concert halls, and the museum, to symbolize the richness and the magnetism of the city. Also, within a few minutes walk are luxury apartments, slums, and the housing projects that try to correct some of the abuses and the indignities of slum life. Not much farther on, one comes upon a street academy, a new approach to educating the dropout and the would-be dropout. How can we mobilize our many urban resources to solve urban problems?

The institute brought together the exponents of different points of view and the advocates of radically different solutions, and gave the participants the opportunity to discuss issues and plans with some of the leaders in urban education. Among the speakers—now the writers of the chapters that follow—are spokesmen for militant communities and militant professionals. Also represented at the institute were those close enough to urban education to understand its problems, yet just far enough removed to be able to see these problems in proper perspective.

We are grateful to the following workshop leaders who contributed so much to the success of the Urban Institute: Mildred K. Lee, Marina Mercado, Dr. Thomas Mulkeen, Marvin Orzak, Adalinda Rodriguez, Adelaide Sanford, Seymour Sternberg, Dr. Alan Sugarman, Edward Wakin, Morris Wallach, and Dr. Alfred Weiss.

The authors are further indebted to Joyce Marcus and Adele Larschan for reviewing the manuscript. We also thank Ann Fallon and Ann Goldstein for typing this manuscript, and George Theodore, representative of Dictaphone, Inc., for donating the audio equipment which facilitated the transcription of each speaker's presentation.

SHELDON MARCUS
HARRY N. RIVLIN

Contents

1 *Education 1980*   3
FRED M. HECHINGER

2 *Compensatory Education*   19
DOXEY A. WILKERSON

3 *Delinquents and Dropouts: Some
Implications for Schools*   40
WILLIAM C. KVARACEUS

4 *New Methods of Teaching the Socially
Disadvantaged*   64
ROBERT A. DENTLER

5 *Moderating Conflicts through School
Public Relations*   79
DOYLE BORTNER

6 *Improving School-Community Relations*   95
ELLIOTT SHAPIRO

7 *Community Control of Schools*   111
REVEREND C. HERBERT OLIVER

8 *Teacher Unionism and Education*   133
ALBERT SHANKER

9 *Education and the Puerto Rican Child*   149
JOSEPH MONSERRAT

10 *Militancy and Violence: A Challenge to Urban Schools*   160
SHELDON MARCUS AND PHILIP D. VAIRO

11 *The Unanswered Questions*   173
HARRY N. RIVLIN

Index   189

Conflicts in Urban Education

1

Education 1980

FRED M. HECHINGER

Not long ago a somewhat daring television program reminded its viewers of the predictions made by the Futurama exhibit at the 1939 World's Fair. It was a bold glance at the future, particularly in urban America. The cities had been turned into soaring Shangri-las with unlimited space for living, recreation, and a gracious existence for all. Gone were the slums. Transportation was speedy and invisible, moving quietly through underground channels. Aboveground, the pedestrian ruled supreme, no longer threatened by automobiles. Gone were the traffic jams, the noise, and the poisonous exhaust fumes. The car of the future itself was safe and beautiful. Pollution had evaporated. Air and water were pure poetry. Needless to say, the futuristic American city knew no strife, no racial conflict, no ugliness in sight or mind.

It is now more than thirty years after these predictions, and there is no need to point out that, as Mort Sahl might say again, the future *still* lies ahead. Slums and strife are still with us, more intolerable than ever; and conditions in the cities are worse than before. Conditions are worse in the streets and in the air, and to millions of straphangers they are worse underground, too. I cite the discrepancies between Futurama 1939 and the urban reality of 1970 merely to underscore the danger of optimistic prophecy. Indeed, the only reason prophets generally get away with their long-range forecasts is that nobody remembers what they said. Newspapermen should be careful not to be prophets; what they predict is indelibly set down in the archives. I would not want copy boys in 1980 to sneer at any futuristic follies of mine.

There is another reason why I have misgivings about peering far into the future. The favorite game at present is to plan for the world of the year 2000. The reason this exercise is so popular is that those who do the planning are reasonably sure that they will not be held responsible at so distant a date. Moreover, it is easy to be bold about a decade or a generation hence, and it often frees one of the dreary and more risky task of being bold about today and tomorrow. Yet, unless we are prepared to face our todays and our tomorrows boldly, the only safe prediction is that the utopian plans for the long run will be delusions riddled by disasters.

And so, the only way I am willing to look ahead to 1980 is in terms of now and next year. The questions that must be asked should focus on the urban problems as we know and see them. They must deal with the future of all children—those of the slums and those of the middle class; those of the minorities that have already "made it" as well as the ones still struggling. Devoid of current slogans and stripped of all name-calling, that of the gutter as well as that of the sociologists, these are the issues.

The immediate temptation is to think of the future in terms of the currently popular and political demands and theories: the debate over "open admission" to colleges regardless of grades, the controversy over community control of the schools, the pros and cons of the establishment of Third World courses and departments, and a host of other, rapidly changing, questions. In fact, none of these touches the heart of the matter; and it is self-defeating to become imprisoned by these issues in an effort to move toward a tolerable, and an eventually dignified and satisfying future for urban education. This course is too narrow to foster sweeping, satisfactory answers.

If we take the narrow view, we may by 1980 have passed from the point of no return to total disaster. We may have moved from urban decay, with its sporadic explosions into violence, to full-scale ethnic warfare. We may be well on the road back to the days when the public schools were merely the schools of the poor. With this would come the stratification of American society that has so severely retarded the progress of other nations and civilizations, and which the American blueprint so emphatically rejected.

We should not be blind to the danger implicit in the narrow view of the racial conflict that has begun to make separatism appear, in the minds of misguided theorists in both the black and the white camps, as a tolerable condition. That danger is clearly one of spreading all-black institutions or black divisions of white institutions (schools as well as colleges) throughout the country. Instead of guiding the Negro colleges of the South toward full integration and institutional greatness, we would be creating new Negro colleges throughout the North, to the satisfaction of racists of either side.

We may, in this dismal process, succumb to the deception that all standards of excellence and of accomplishment are nothing but "middle-class values" and therefore meaningless, irrelevant and corrupt, to be shed like a snake's skin at the start of a better spring. This would mean that we would move from the neglect and miseducation of the past (which denied decent employment opportunities to great masses of underpriv-

ileged youth) to a kind of surrender—the surrender to those
who maintain that the rigors of education and training are
nothing but an aberration of middle-class life.

If we proceed on such a course, we may be able to reduce
education to an existentialist togetherness. True, this would
eliminate all failures because in the absence of goals there can
be no yardstick of progress. But it would turn our society, with
all its economic and social obligations, into a permanent summer camp of self-centered and asocial adolescents. This clearly
would not only reduce the productive potential of American
society, and with it the ability to reduce want and poverty, in
the long run, but it would also almost certainly increase the
power of a small, privileged group that would soon command a
monopoly of skills and technological know-how. In the worst
instances, such social orders tend to descend to an alliance
between the least qualified rabble and the overprivileged
manipulators of production and power. This is the classic
pattern of the fascist state. In short, the course I consider so
dangerous is one that would delight all the racists and reac-
tionaries who have always sneered at real educational opportunities for all.

It would obviously be futile to take part in a discussion on
the future of urban education if I thought so tragic a course
were inevitable. On the contrary, I am certain that an urban
revival is still possible within the next decade, in which public
education must play the key role.

I stress *public* education because I am firmly convinced that
there can be no effective substitute for it. I view as deceptive
those currently fashionable schemes which would rely on
private nongovernmental efforts to cure educational deficiencies. This is not to say that private schools and institutions of
higher education cannot, indeed, must not, carry out experimental programs to help improve the educational process. On
the contrary, such pioneering efforts as those illustrated by
Harlem Prep, the street academies, and many other privately

supported institutions and movements are imperative. They infuse new ideas into the public institutions. They give courage and inspiration to thousands of dedicated men and women in the public schools who are frustrated and disheartened by the lack of imagination in the school system. But the purpose of these private ventures remains to improve, not to circumvent public education.

The basic answers to the public school problems are not to be found in radical, new miracle cures; nor are they to be found in educational technology, useful though it may be. There is not even much need for new research on basic strategies. We know, beyond doubt, that two factors are essential in dealing successfully with young children: an early start and the personal attention of a competent and sympathetic adult. I stress the case of young children because we must get away from the need for compensatory education.

Although we know this, the public education systems, especially in our big cities, have done little to translate this knowledge into action. While we have tried to alleviate the problem through Project Head Start, the programs are still nothing more than a band-aid to cope with a major epidemic. Anybody familiar with life in the urban slums knows that until extensive, early child care and preschool attention can be brought to these children, and that unless this care is consistent, the problems will persist.

Our claim for the need of research into this business is nothing short of ridiculous. The Scandinavians have been implementing for decades what we are still debating in pseudo-educational jargon. They have made available well-supervised infant day care centers for working mothers, often attached to the factories themselves. The Russians, too, provide nurseries for children from age two and they permit parents to deposit their children as early as seven o'clock in the morning and to leave them there until the early evening. They provide three well-balanced meals for those who want and need them, and if necessary, the children may even stay overnight in supervised dormitories.

In the examples I cited in Scandinavia and Russia, the day care centers are voluntary. In Scandinavia they are voluntary and free; in Russia, voluntary and not free. The parents must pay a fee but on a level scaled to their income, and at a rather low level. The Soviets also have an intermediate approach called "Schools of the Extended Day" in which the children can stay after class until as late as seven o'clock in the evening to do their homework and to have some supervised recreational activities. Another example of a nonvoluntary program is the kibbutz education in Israel. Preschool education is not voluntary there, because it is the only possibility of education in a community where everyone works. I would prefer to see voluntary preschool education here, despite the dangers that sometimes these centers would fail those people most in need of this service because they were ignorant of it. But I believe it is important to let the parents decide at what level and at what time they can take care of their children. In a Russian preschool nursery, a parent who is able to care for his child after work may pick him up at four o'clock. If the parent thinks it would be better to leave the child until after supper, that is all right.

Critics have maintained that care is substituted for love in those day care centers. In answer, I would like to relate an experience I had in Russia. After I had spent the day in one of the preschool centers—a nursery school in a worker settlement in a suburban area of Moscow—a woman, the director, said to me:

You know, I had to call all my parents together the other day to lecture to them. I told them that I know that every night when they pick up their children, most of them bring toys and candy. I know why they bring them toys and candy. It isn't because they love them that much, it is because they feel guilty because they have left them with us all day.

The problem is a universal one. Of course, those parents really did love the children. My observations in the Soviet Union and in the Scandinavian centers was that there is expert and frequently loving care of the children. If you have the choice of letting the child spend the day in a well-ordered and constructive environment or of leaving him uncared for in a slum, you must take him out of the slum. It struck me every time I visited Ocean Hill-Brownsville, that, even where progress was being made in the schools, once out of the school there is still the terrible environment, the desolate blocks, and the uncared for young. This is not a good way for any child to spend even part of the day.

It is difficult to apply the Scandinavian success to American society. The Scandinavian countries have the advantage of a very homogeneous society and a society without the slum problems we face here. This objection does not apply to the Soviet Union. They do have minority problems—different from ours, but very sizable ones in terms of the many different nationalities within its borders. But even more pertinent is the fact that, the Soviet Union faces urbanization problems very similar to ours. One of the great problems in the large Soviet cities, particularly Moscow and Leningrad (not unlike New York, Chicago and San Francisco), is the influx of people from the educationally disadvantaged rural areas. When reading about the Soviet education system in the cities, keep in mind that much of what happens there has not yet spread to the rural and outlying areas. There has been an enormous influx of the illiterate or semiliterate from the rural population which has created problems similar to those in America's cities. The Soviet problem is not as acute, because being a directed society, it can take drastic preventive steps that would be unacceptable to an open society. For instance, it simply declares certain cities "closed," and you cannot move there unless you either have a job waiting for you or someone wants to marry you. You can slow the influx, but the problem still exists. Yet, even with these somewhat lesser urban problems, these societies have resorted to the far more extensive use of the schools than we have done.

The traditional American reaction to preschool centers has been that they interfere with the sanctity of home and family. This argument may or may not be valid in the case of middle-class families—at least, there is room for argument. But for the children of the urban slums, such objections are sheer nonsense. The sooner and the more completely they are weaned away from the debilitating environment that destroys them both before and after their school years, the greater the hope of leading them to true equality of opportunity.

This same need to place children in a wholesome environment is true of class size, particularly for the ages of from two through nine. Good private schools, drawing the majority of their enrollment from highly privileged homes, provide one adult for no more than eight children. Yet classes in the public schools, even in the most difficult neighborhoods, struggle along with three or four times as many youngsters per teacher.

The answer given as to why this problem remains insoluble is that the taxpayer cannot afford to double or triple the staffing of our public schools.

This is, of course, quite true, just as it is true that urban education cannot be substantially changed within the confines of a system-defined and union-ordered day of nine to three. The answer must clearly be found in new arrangements and in a totally different deployment of personnel. Unless highly trained and carefully selected teaching specialists—paid on generous professional scales—can be augmented by large armies of carefully selected and supervised nonprofessionals, there is no hope that 1980 will be better than 1970.

These armies of support forces would be readily available but for resistance by short-sighted conservatism. It is a sad commentary on the inflexibility of American public education that the concept of the teacher aide, introduced in the early 1950's by the now defunct Fund for the Advancement of Education of the Ford Foundation, has had to struggle against irrational opposition and disinterest. Almost two decades later, the idea is still only gaining limited support when it ought to be a major force in the reform of the public schools.

My observations in Ocean Hill-Brownsville last year confirmed my belief in the effectiveness of paraprofessionals, especially in underprivileged areas. It not only permits saturation staffing; it brings into the schools the warmth and the authority of the neighborhood; it creates a bridge between classroom and home, a bridge that alone can span the terrible gap of suspicion with which slum parents view the school as the local agent of a distant and incomprehensible system; and it brings useful employment to women who otherwise would find little opportunity to take part in this essential process of community upgrading.

I witnessed the startling success of an experimental Bereiter-Engleman project for the preschool education of seventy-five Ocean Hill-Brownsville youngsters. The only reason the experiment succeeded so magnificently is that there was a regular adult supervisor for every five or six youngsters. Only three of the adults were licensed teachers; the others were neighborhood women who had been trained in a summer crash program. The level of achievement acquired by these children in reading and arithmetic is proof of the success of the project. I challenge middle-class communities to compare the academic accomplishments of their five year olds against those of these seventy-five presumably disadvantaged children.

The method is highly structured. This, in theory, offends many of the early childhood experts who support more traditional programs. Highly structured systems, they claim, risk suppressing creativity and self-expression. I think the experimenters and the people who devised the experiment felt that these objections were largely based on the traditional approach to very secure children from sheltered homes. By contrast in the slum environment, this method succeeded for three reasons. First, the children were always given to understand what they would have to do to succeed. They learned to cope with what was in front of them and also to cope with the next step. Much of the early reading is directly aimed at enabling children to read instructions, thus eliminating the worry of remembering the teacher's instructions. The top of the sheet says: "Do such and such." "Raise you hand at such and such a point." Some of the words that were dealt with in the early stages were ones the children used frequently, such as *paper bag, container, blackboard* and so forth.

The security this gave the children was one positive aspect of the program. They knew exactly what they were responsible for, and could proceed step by step, understanding exactly what had been accomplished at each step.

Second, and equally important, they progressed under the close personal supervision of an adult who knew exactly what to do. There were never more than six children with this one adult.

Third, because the method was so clearly defined, the teacher was explicitly told what to do next and how to do it. In this fashion, hastily trained adults could be used, providing the children had confidence in them and they liked the children. In addition, there were supervising teachers available who made sure nothing was misinterpreted.

My observation was that one possibly objectional feature— standardization—did not result in the children being repressed. They were happy to show what they could do. Since nobody was left to straggle behind, there was no sense of insecurity. After the required reading, writing, and mathematics, the children would go into another part of the room, draw funny pictures on the blackboards, and do all the normal, creative preschool and nursery school activities. Thus, they were not pressed into a long academic day. But the security of knowing that they could do what was expected encouraged them to like school.

They were not just reading words; they were reading what would help communicate with their teachers.

Another lesson for the road to a livable 1980 was driven home by the Ocean Hill-Brownsville experience. During the crisis of the general school strike and the walkout of many of the regular teachers from the schools of the demonstration district, considerable numbers of young men from the elite colleges and even the professional schools were hired to fill the vacuum. These sixty-day wonders, trained hastily by the schools of education of local universities, were not given a kindly reception by the establishment forces. To the extent that they were strike breakers, from the viewpoint of the union and the administrators, that attitude was entirely understandable. These men were sneered at as draft dodgers (which they were) even by those union teachers who shared a contempt for the futile war in Vietnam. It was asserted that these volunteers had no lasting commitment to the public schools and would leave as soon as the crisis was over. This was largely true, as was the charge that many of them had been attracted by a political rather than an educational commitment.

Not discounting these objections, the fact remains that many of these young men, despite their often glaring lack of preparation, were remarkably successful, particularly with the younger children. Much of their success was undoubtedly due to the fact that they were men. The lower grades are traditionally staffed largely by women. Moreover, they were *young* men, filled with a combination of idealism and a sense of personal security that may have been the result of their very privilege—personal and educational.

Two years ago, there was a slow trickle of instructors from the National Teacher Corps into the public schools of New York City. The professional reaction to these young teachers was very much like that accorded to the young people teaching in Ocean Hill-Brownsville. They were looked down upon as nonprofessional. They were not committed to a lifetime of teaching, and, therefore, not bound by the professional codes of teachers.

The hostility was so strong that, when *The New York Times* reported on a group of these teachers who were doing a very creditable job in a school in Queens, a letter from the principal and the staff of that school charged that it had been implied that these people knew something that the regular staff did not know.[1] My answer to that was, "Yes, they do know something that the regular staff does not know. They know that they are not a part of the system."

If there is any validity to having this kind of influx, it is to have people who are not part of the system keep the system in flux. It has recently been proposed that the police bring in short-term "civilians." One of the very few points in favor of the draft as a system of military service is the influx of civilian draftees. It is safer than having to rely wholly on an entirely professional army.

Some teachers hold that new temporary teachers are familiar with drugs and may introduce them into the schools. Drugs are a very real danger, both in and out of the schools. I do not think, however, that the influx of young volunteers poses more of a danger than the influx of regular young teachers. They are all of the same generation and background.

Let me add one very specific example to this. In one of my visits to JHS 271, while there were still barricades around the school, I sat in a classroom during a lesson on Afro-American history. The class was conducted by a very capable young man who was one of the "sixty-day wonders." Halfway through the session he threw the class open to a very interesting, and spirited discussion. One boy was extremely bright, though not terribly articulate. He obviously had more drive and ideas, was more concerned than his classmates—to the point that he thought he was offending me. And he probably wanted to

[1] *New York Times*, March 6, 1967, Letter to the editor.

offend me. After the class, the teacher spoke to me and called my attention to this boy whom he considered to have tremendous potential, although he was educationally badly retarded. He had come to know him quite well and, trying to help him, had found out that during the summer vacation the youngster had started to mix with dangerous elements in the local drug culture. The teacher was doing everything he could to get this pupil away from drugs. About half a year later, the boy had become a student leader. He had given up the drugs.

My point is that it is very dangerous to create stereotypes. If you pick good people, who are concerned with the welfare of children, it is safe to assume that they will not be part-time dope pushers. The fact that such recruits are not going to remain in teaching for more than a year or two should not obscure the essential lesson: they succeeded in winning the children's, and often the parents', confidence and attention.

If we can mobilize an army of successful classroom temporaries, why not do it on a regular, recurring basis? The idea of the Peace Corps was not discarded because the young people who are anxious to devote two years of their lives to such service would not make this mission permanently a career, or because they were unschooled in some of the ways of career diplomats.

The fact is that enthusiasm is a priceless ingredient in staffing the slum schools; but it is equally true that enthusiasm cannot be readily preserved. It is often lacking in the most competent career teachers. The common-sense solution, then, is to abolish the draft, with its inequities, to a form of truly universal national service, similar to the Peace Corps, which would channel the idealism of the young into such essential missions as staffing the slum schools.

Teaching, perhaps more than any other profession (because the rate of turnover is greater) draws an increasing influx of young people. This in itself assures the flow of new ideas and lessens the conservatism of the system. The impact of the influx of this new, change-oriented brood into the established professional organization, the National Education Association, even over the short period since the mid-1950s, is startling. For instance, immediately after the 1954 Supreme Court decision, the stand of the NEA on school desegregation was almost entirely the traditional, Southern approach. "Leave things alone." "Wait until people reform in their hearts." This position has been completely reversed. The NEA has given ultimatums rigorously enforcing the desegregation guidelines established by the Civil Rights Acts.

And the same is true of the influence of the young classroom teachers on the NEA. I cite this as an example of the possibility that the influx of young people, more attuned to the problems we confront, will bring about the kind of new professionalism we need. This is not to say that there was no professionalism in teaching in the past, but rather that it was a conservative professionalism similar to that practised by such organizations as the American Medical Association.

The tripartite approach (that is, a regular army of highly qualified and highly paid professional teachers and administrators, a support force of community-based paraprofessionals and a continuing influx of idealistic young college graduates, regardless of their permanent career plans) would not only permit saturation staffing, it would also foster a diversity of personnel that has been lacking in the conventional table of organization. An inevitable byproduct would be the creation of a large segment of the general citizenry with a firsthand knowledge of the problems of the urban schools and the needs of public education.

Here we should reiterate the desperate urgency to improve the training of the regular teaching staff and to create a system of internship and unsentimental weeding of the ill-suited or incompetent along the lines prescribed by James B. Conant almost a decade ago, but ignored by much of the education establishment. The time to move in that direction is now when the teacher shortage is virtually at an end, and the salary scales have at last begun to be professional.

Along with these reforms, however, another priority must be considered: the rapid induction of great numbers of well-educated and competent young people from the currently underprivileged ethnic minorities (Negro, Puerto Rican, Mexican-American, and so on) into the ranks of teaching and school administration. This, I firmly believe, is far more vital than the issue of Afro-American studies that is monopolizing so much attention on the campuses and in the headlines. These studies are important as part of an understanding of American history; but it would be a great disservice to future public education if what is currently popular and politically attractive were to delay the training of a great number of Negro teachers of English, mathematics, science, languages, and other disciplines.

At the same time, it is imperative that able young minority members be promoted rapidly to positions of leadership and influence. This is not an unprecedented approach. In an emergency, the traditional routes are often discarded to attain the desired goals. The rapid promotion of air force officers to general rank during World War II was both opposed and ridiculed by the more conventional army and navy establishment, but it was clearly in the national interest. Today, the use of the public schools as a major avenue to upgrade the socioeconomic status of the disadvantaged minorities is equally in the national as well as in the educational interest.

These (in condensed form) are the major steps which, in my opinion, could assure that 1980 will mark a milestone of educational accomplishment in urban America. Obviously, this does not mean that the many details omitted are not of great importance. For example, to overlook the potential of the educational technology as a tool in the hands of the professional, as well as of the paraprofessional and temporary teachers, is to exclude education from the benefits of scientific achievement. It is absurd to allow television, which (even in its currently perverted and inane manifestations) has been so compelling an influence on generations of children, to remain in the periphery. It is equally as absurd to permit computerized instruction, automated libraries and a host of already developed teaching instruments to remain the underexploited oddities that they are today. These are issues that can and should be tackled by more qualified experts than I, in cooperation with education, industry and government.

What I have tried to sketch may not be a hopeful picture— not because reforms are impossible but because past experience has so often shown the establishment and the profession to be extremely slow and irresponsibly reluctant in bringing about real change; change initiated through the initiative of the professionally informed rather than through the angry pressures by the dissatisfied and disaffected.

The solutions I have suggested are educationally rather than politically radical, and I submit that continued educational conservatism will dangerously aggravate the political pressures. Those pressures would inevitably turn against public education itself, as they already have against lumbering, unresponsible urban public education systems. It is unreasonable to expect an educational utopia either in 1980 or at any time. But it is entirely reasonable to predict that the urban schools in 1980 will either be accomplices to urban disaster or partners in an urban renaissance. Which it will be will be determined by the actions we take, not ten years from now, but this year and next.

2

Compensatory Education

DOXEY A. WILKERSON

The burgeoning movement called compensatory education is a recent development around an old problem. Although the public schools have always had large numbers of low-achieving pupils, mainly from impoverished backgrounds, not until the 1960s were major and widespread educational programs addressed especially to their needs. Previously, there had been occasional discussions about "slow learners" in professional journals and conferences dealing with presumed individual deviations from normal classroom behavior, but such terms as *culturally deprived* or *socially disadvantaged* children and *compensatory education* were not current.

Now, however, compensatory education for the disadvantaged is a dominant theme in the profession and, indeed, in general public discussion. Major attention is given to it in educational journals and conferences and the general press; and vast numbers of varied compensatory programs—from preschool through college—are being developed by federal, state, and local public school authorities, together with a wide range of foundations and other private agencies. It is important to note that the main dynamics of this movement lie not in recent deterioration in the school performance of lower-class children, but in recent developments in the economic, social, and political life of the country.

The Emergence of Compensatory Education

The main targets of the new programs of compensatory education are children of the poor from the urban and rural slums. Most of them are Negroes, but they also include large numbers of Puerto Ricans and Mexican-Americans and Indians together with substantial numbers of poor whites. The incidence of academic retardation among these children is high, and they tend to drop out of school when the compulsory attendance age limit is reached.

It should be emphasized, however, that the educational problems of poor children today are no worse—indeed, they are probably less acute—than those of countless numbers of poor children attending public schools two or three generations ago. Read Jane Addams on the plight of Italian immigrants in the schools of Chicago, or Jacob Riis on the schools of New York City's Lower East Side. The patterns of academic frustration and failure which they describe sound markedly like those predominating in our literature on compensatory education today. Descendants of these early immigrant families often ask: "Why can't the Negroes and Puerto Ricans make it in school?" adding, "We, too, were poor; but we made it." Their perceptions are distorted by nostalgia. They probably do not realize, for example, that even as late as the 1920s the big-city dropout rate was 80 percent, more than twice as large as it is today.

The big difference between today and yesterday is not in the academic performance of impoverished children, but in the opportunity structure of the world of work. At that earlier stage in our country's history, the economy was at a much lower level of technological development and was expanding rapidly, creating more and more jobs for unskilled workers. Young people with little formal education found abundant opportunities for employment and for upward mobility in the society. Today's economy, however, is expanding much more slowly, and its high level of technology affords fewer and fewer job opportunities for young people with less than a high school education. School dropouts today, especially if they are black, generally become a part of that growing population of the chronically unemployed, with no perspective other than continuing poverty and the social degradation that is its usual correlate.

A high school education or better is almost a prerequisite for coping with the demands of today's economy and the complex urban-industrial society that now prevails. This is something "new" in our society. Because of it, the failure of our schools to educate large proportions of the poor adequately, especially Negroes, has given rise to social and political movements which constitute the main dynamics of compensatory education.

Confronted with school experiences which foredoomed their youth to poverty and degradation, and armed with the 1954 decision of the Supreme Court, the Negro people, together with important allies, united in the early 1960s to develop a powerful movement for school integration. They were convinced, with good cause, that segregated schools were grossly inferior, and operated severely to restrict the opportunities of Negro youth. The corrective was seen as having their children attend "white" schools, where education proceeded on a much higher level. But their demands for school integration were generally countered by proposals for compensatory education.

During the early 1960s I made a study of *School Segregation and Integration in the North* for the National Association of

Intergroup Relations Officials. In cities all across the country, the Negro communities were united in agitation for school integration; instead, most school officials offered markedly to improve the segregated Negro schools in the ghetto—through increased personnel, smaller classes, specially designed programs, improved facilities and equipment, almost anything short of integrating the schools. In a very real sense (much as in the South while "The Segregation Cases" were before the federal courts) compensatory education emerged in the North as an off-target response to the movement for school integration. It sought to solve the problem of noneducation in the ghetto, and at the same time to circumvent integration, by developing special programs for the "culturally deprived" in segregated ghetto schools.

Noneducation in the Ghetto

This noneducation is especially prevalent among minority group children of the poor. Suggestive of its dimensions, both qualitative and quantitative, are a few facts from an analysis I made recently of the status of Negroes and Puerto Ricans in the New York City public schools.

Probably the most critical academic problem is the excessively high incidence of reading retardation among Negro and Puerto Rican pupils as compared with other pupils. Illustrative are data for two groups of public schools in the Bronx: fifty-three "ghetto schools" in which Negroes and Puerto Ricans constitute 95 percent of the enrollment, and nineteen "non-ghetto schools" where white pupils account for 83 percent of the enrollment. Comparisons are made of the performance on 1967 city-wide reading tests of pupils in combined grades four through nine: 31,871 pupils in the "ghetto schools" and 10,254 pupils in the "non-ghetto schools." They reveal, among other things, that in these grades:

1. Pupils reading at or above grade level constitute only 10 percent of the total in the "ghetto schools," but 65 percent of the total in the "non-ghetto schools"

2. Pupils retarded in reading by three months to three years include 66 percent of those in the "ghetto schools," but only 29 percent of those in the "non-ghetto schools"

3. Pupils retarded in reading by three years to five years account for 23 percent of those in the "ghetto schools," but only 6 percent of those in the "non-ghetto" schools

A somewhat similar comparison of intermediate and junior high schools in the Bronx in 1968 reveals that among the twelve predominantly (76 percent or more) Negro and Puerto Rican schools, none had more than 40 percent of its pupils reading at or above the eighth-grade level; whereas among the four predominantly (76 percent or more) white schools, all had more than 70 percent of their pupils reading at or above the eighth-grade level.

Here evident (in the basic tool of reading) are gross differences in the quality of education for mainly impoverished Negro and Puerto Rican children and that for predominantly middle-class white children in the Bronx. Such differences are known to prevail in most other parts of the New York City public school system.

This prevailing noneducation of impoverished Negro and Puerto Rican children is also evident in many other indices. To cite only a few: In New York City as a whole, approximately 57 percent of tenth-grade Negro and Puerto Rican pupils drop out of school before grade twelve, as compared with only about 16 percent of other children. Among the City's academic and special high schools, there are nine where Negro and Puerto Rican students constitute 75 percent or more of the total, and twenty-eight where the enrollment is 75 percent or more white. The diplomas awarded by these two groups of schools in June

1968 included 69 percent "general" diplomas and only 22 percent "academic" diplomas in the predominantly Negro and Puerto Rican high schools, as compared with 56 percent "academic" diplomas and only 32 percent "general" diplomas in the predominantly white high schools. (The remainder are accounted for by "commercial" and other types of diplomas.) In other words, more than two-thirds of the graduates of the predominantly Negro and Puerto Rican high schools received little more than certificates of attendance, the "General" diploma that has no status with college admissions officials or with most employers. In contrast, most graduates of the predominantly white high schools received the standard "Academic" diploma, which is the required "passport" to higher education and desirable employment.

Relatively few Negro and Puerto Rican students are enrolled in New York City's four-year public colleges. In September 1967, they constituted a substantial proportion of the total enrollments in several two-year community colleges—for example, Manhattan Community College, 30 percent; Bronx Community College, 39 percent; and New York City Community College, 36 percent. In the degree-granting institutions, however, comparatively very few Negro and Puerto Rican students were enrolled. They accounted for only 5 percent of the total at Brooklyn College, 11 percent at City College - Uptown, 7 percent at Hunter College - Bronx, 10 percent at Hunter College - Park, and 5 percent at Queens College.

To summarize: Negro and Puerto Rican children in our public schools do not learn to read nearly as well as other children, which necessarily handicaps them in all other areas of the curriculum. They have a greater tendency to drop out after reaching the "school-leaving age" of sixteen. Relatively few of those who graduate from high school receive the standard academic diploma, which is essential for admission to college and to most fields of satisfying employment. And they are grossly underrepresented among students attending public, degree-granting institutions of higher education. Taken together, these facts suggest that noneducation is the prevailing norm for Puerto Rican and Negro young people in New York City.

Most of these youngsters come from backgrounds of poverty and racial discrimination. The failure of our schools to educate them means that their perspectives consist mainly of limited personal development, chronic unemployment, poverty and dependency, and the likelihood of falling prey to the many evils that infest the urban ghetto.

It is to this prevailing pattern of noneducation among the children of the poor that compensatory education is avowedly addressed, but its accomplishments fall far short of its promises.

Failure among Compensatory Programs

Probably the earliest of the "new" compensatory education programs was the Demonstration Guidance Project which began in the late 1950s at Manhattan's Junior High School 43. This was extended during the early 1960s into the widespread, much "watered-down" Higher Horizons Program. Other comprehensive, large-scale compensatory programs during the early 1960s were developed as part of the Great Cities School Improvement Program, sponsored by the Ford Foundation in eighteen metropolitan centers. When the northern school-integration movement reached its peak in 1963–1964, compensatory programs were begun in large and small cities across the country. Their further extension and development was hastened by unprecedented financial support from the federal government, mainly for Head Start, Title I, and Upward Bound programs. Public school systems, colleges and universities, and hosts of other agencies joined in the movement. A vast literature on the "culturally deprived" or "socially disadvantaged" child quickly emerged; within a few years compensatory education had developed into the most dynamic sector of American education.

I have visited scores of these programs in most parts of the country, and have been impressed by the dedication and enthusiasm of most staff personnel, especially by their high appraisals of their programs: all are doing "fine work"; pupils are "progressing rapidly"; the programs are a "big success." Systematic research evaluations, however, generally tell a somewhat different story.

Measured outcomes of compensatory programs suggest that some of them are, indeed, effective in remedying the educational deficiencies of underprivileged children. This is generally true of the preschool programs, including most Head Start projects, even though the gains there reported tend to disappear when pupils enter the regular school programs. It is also true of the programs for higher education. Upward Bound, for example, seems to be largely responsible for the entrance into college of some 8,000 to 10,000 disadvantaged youth—who, incidentally, tend to maintain scholastic averages equal to those of their more advantaged classmates, and whose dropout rate is far lower than that of college students generally. Scattered throughout the country, especially on the elementary school level, there are many individual compensatory projects which also show substantial improvement in the academic performance of disadvantaged children. Thus, it is not accurate to generalize, as is increasingly being done in the literature, that "compensatory education has failed." Some compensatory programs are succeeding, and that fact is very important.

It is true, however, that most large-scale, comprehensive programs of compensatory education are failing substantially to improve the academic achievement of disadvantaged children. When such programs are subjected to careful research, the most common finding is that they made "no significant difference" in the education of poor children. This was the finding for New York City's Higher Horizon Program, the Philadelphia School Improvement Program, the Banneker

Project in St. Louis, and (although not reported publicly) the other "Great Cities" programs. The New York City More Effective Schools program—which I think has great potential— has been shown to produce a statistically significant improvement in pupils' achievement in reading and mathematics; but even here, the measured differences are too slight to be assessed as educationally significant.

About three years ago, the U.S. Commission on Civil Rights compared the academic achievement of Negro children in large compensatory programs in the segregated ghetto schools of several cities with that of children from similarly disadvantaged backgrounds who were bussed out of the ghetto to white schools for purposes of integration. The Commission found that the ghetto children who attended integrated schools *without compensatory programs* were achieving better in school than their peers who attended segregated schools *with compensatory programs*. Thus, as regards the goal of improved academic achievement, it would seem that the school integration demands of the Negro people in the early 1960s were more valid than the compensatory programs they were given.

It is fair to generalize that although some programs of compensatory education appear to be effective, especially those on the preschool and college-preparatory levels, most of the large-scale, comprehensive programs seem to have failed significantly to improve the academic performance of disadvantaged pupils. The causes of this failure have not been conclusively determined, but there is ample basis for informed speculation about them.

Why Compensatory Programs Commonly Fail

Educators have traditionally attributed the high incidence of academic retardation and failure in slum schools to characteristics of the pupils. Children from the slums were believed to be "poorly endowed by nature." Although modern behavioral science has effectively disproved the hypothesis of racial and social-class differences in the inheritance of intellectual ability, occasionally atavistic behavioral scientists still appear to reassert this hoary doctrine. The more generally accepted current explanation, however, is that children from the ghetto have been so scarred by primary socialization under conditions of poverty and discrimination that their potential for cognitive development is severely limited. They are said to be "culturally deprived" or "socially disadvantaged."

This "cultural deprivation" hypothesis is now dominant in professional thought on the education of children from impoverished backgrounds. More than any other doctrine, it defines the theoretical orientation of compensatory education—it undertakes to "make-up" for presumed inadequacies in the preschool development of the child. Inherent in this doctrine, however, is probably the basic explanation of the widespread failure of schools to educate the children of the poor; it leads to defeatist attitudes and nonadaptive school procedures.

Consider some of the implications of this "cultural deprivation" thesis, and especially the educational practices it tends to foster.

First, children from the ghetto are perceived as sharing a common set of characteristics, much as if they came from the same mold. The literature on compensatory education repeatedly asserts that "these children" come from impoverished backgrounds which afford little opportunity for intellectual development—broken homes, uneducated parents or guardians with no concern for the education of their children, no books or newspapers, narrow and barren environmental settings, and the like. Consequently, they enter school largely "nonverbal," with atrocious language patterns, and lacking the experiential basis for effective cognitive development. It is said, further, that their learning style is motor rather than verbal, concrete rather than abstract; that they have little or no future-orientation, but seek immediate gratifications; and that their aspiration level is low and their academic motivation almost nil.

There is much wrong with this description, including demonstrable factual errors. However, the main weakness is that it stereotypes; it obscures the reality of human variation. Poverty *is* a common bond, but "the poor" are still a heterogeneous population. There are intact families, as well as broken homes; upwardly mobile families, as well as those hopelessly mired in dependency; nuclear and extended families which provide love and security and encourage educational development, as well as families whose impact on the young is mainly negative. And ghetto children, like all children, are wondrously varied human beings—in self-concept, interpersonal relations, academic ability, motivation and probable future. To perceive these children in terms of a derogatory stereotype tends not only to thwart theoretical clarity, but also to promote pedantic and sterile educational practices.

Second, the premise of cultural deprivation carries a heavy overtone of doubt that the children of the poor are capable of effective learning. Although it is impolitic to claim they are "innately inferior" (aloud, that is), sociological determinism provides a rationale that is equally as damning. To allege, as some educators do, that "these children" enter school bereft of the experiential background and the motivation essential to cope with academic tasks is simply to deny their ability to learn; and this necessarily affects the behavior of both teachers and learners.

Teachers who do not believe that impoverished children can attain the achievement goals expected of other children will behave toward them differently—in the learning objectives they set, in the help and encouragement they give, and in the standards of performance they accept. Morever, either explicitly or subtly, these assessments are inevitably communicated to their pupils, who, in turn, tend to adapt their behavior to what they perceive as the teachers' expectations. These relationships were demonstrated experimentally by Davidson and Lang almost a decade ago, and more recently by Rosenthal and Jacobson in their study, *Pygmalion in the Classroom.*

I have come to believe, on the basis of widespread observations and abundant evidence, that an extraordinarily large proportion of the people in our profession seriously doubt the potential of socially disadvantaged children for normal school achievement, especially if they are black. If my perception is substantially correct, then the well-known "self-fulfilling prophecy" seriously limits the academic development of these children.

The tragedy of this tendency is that it is quite unwarranted. It is true that most children from impoverished environments do enter school less advanced educationally than more privileged children, and that they are "harder to teach"—especially when using methods and materials designed for middle-class children. But there is no valid reason to assume that these "handicaps" *preclude* effective learning. Indeed, there is considerable empirical evidence to the contrary. The children of the poor *do* learn effectively when guided in appropriate learning experiences.

Illustrative of this is the dramatic growth achieved in such preschool programs as those conducted by Deutsch and his associates in New York City, by Bereiter and Engelman at the University of Illinois and elsewhere, at the Perry School Project in Ypsilanti, and in many of the Head Start projects. I.Q. gains of between 10 and 20 points are common in such programs and the fact that much of the gain is lost when children enter the regular grades tells us more about the inadequacy of our schools than about the learning ability of the children.

Another example is a special demonstration project conducted by Drs. Kenneth and Mayme Clark at the Northside Center for Child Development several summers ago. Working with educationally retarded children from the Harlem slums, just one hour a day, five days a week, for four weeks, they were able to effect remarkable improvement in reading achievement: an average gain of eight months on a standard reading test and a minimum gain of four months. During the school year that followed, with the children attending all day for nine months, test results at the end showed that the average child among them had gained nothing in reading achievement. These were the same children, so their contrasting performance at Northside and in elementary school cannot be explained in terms of *their* limitations. The explanation must be found in the difference in their learning experiences in the two settings.

The ability of impoverished children to learn effectively when they are taught effectively is further illustrated by many other successful projects here and there about the country. Attention has already been called to Upward Bound. Another at about the same age level is the Harlem Preparatory School, which recruits black adolescents who are failing in high school or have already dropped out, involves them in relevant and meaningful studies under the guidance of dedicated and empathetic teachers, and develops in the process an excitement about learning that none could have predicted on the basis of these students' performances in high school. Harlem Prep's graduates are admitted to prestige colleges throughout the country, where they prove to be good students.

In addition to these special programs, there are scores of individual teachers in New York City schools who manage somehow to elicit better-than-average achievement from pupils from the ghetto. There are also a few elementary schools serving ghetto neighborhoods whose pupils consistently rank high in the city-wide testing program. The pupils involved are no less disadvantaged than those who fail under other teachers or in other schools. Why, then, are such results so rare among schools serving poverty populations—in compensatory as well as conventional programs?

I emphasize this question of negative teacher-expectations because I think it points to one of the main reasons for the prevailing failure of our schools to educate the children of the poor. The negative ideas and attitudes about impoverished children that teachers and school supervisors normally take from the racist and social-class prejudices of our culture have now been reinforced by the widespread ideology of "cultural deprivation."

Third, the inappropriateness of prevailing curricular materials and experiences is another influence militating against effective learning by impoverished children. I refer not only to the absurdity of "Dick and Jane," who are symptomatic. Nor do I imply merely the need for "Black Studies," to which a new approach is overdue. I refer, rather, to the more general irrelevance of our curricular prescriptions to the lives of children from the ghetto.

It is curious that professional literature is filled with treatises on the great differences between the cultural backgrounds and preschool learnings of lower- and middle-class children, yet pupils from the ghetto are confronted with the same curricular materials and experiences we designed for more affluent youngsters. This is "keeping school," not teaching. It violates a pedagogical principle long enshrined in our textbooks on education: that school learning experiences should be appropriate to the background, interests and current stage of development of the learners.

The problem is by no means unique to schools serving the poor. Middle-class children could also profit from curricular experiences that are more relevant to the real world. Most of them, however, have been socialized to accommodate to what the school offers. Moreover, their homes provide educational resources to compensate for inadequacies in the school. Neither of these conditions obtain with most children from the ghetto. For them, good teaching in school is absolutely essential.

The early experiences of a beginning teacher and friend of mine illustrate an approach to making the curriculum relevant to children of the poor. She is a mature person, white, and a resident of Bedford-Stuyvesant. Although a college graduate, she had never been exposed to our professional courses in education. An emergency vacancy in mid-year led to her appointment to teach fourth grade in a school in her neighborhood. All of her pupils were Negroes and poor.

Very early she noticed pupils calling one another "black," then a term of derogation—before the days of "Black is beautiful"—and one target of the epithet complained to the teacher: "Mrs. Smith, he called me black. I'm not black, am I?" Rather than shy away from this situation uncomfortably, as I have seen other white teachers do, she met it head-on. The complaining pupil was called to the front of the room to compare her skin color with a black book; and, of course, they did not match. Then she compared her own hand with a piece of white paper; again, no match. Neither was the pupil "black" nor the teacher "white."

Exploring the question further, she had the whole class stand against the wall, hands outstretched, and organized in an array from the darkest to the lightest skin. There was quite a range, and the question naturally arose: "Why?" From that point on she had them; here was a question that made sense.

Mrs. Smith proceeded from this situation to a series of learning experiences I can only summarize here. There was an explanation, without technical terminology, of why people's skin colors vary. The discussion led them to Africa, and interesting bits of its history and culture. It led to the slave trade, and to many events in the history of Negro Americans. In the course of it all, there was much reading—of special "trade books" the teacher acquired, and, even more, of compositions the pupils dictated and she reproduced in writing. There were also discussions and writing, map work, number work, science, social studies, art and music—all stemming from the name-calling incident and centering around the broader theme of the story of black folk.

For some reason this class of fourth-graders became excited

about the story of John Brown's raid on Harper's Ferry, and they decided to plan their scheduled assembly program around this event. This meant "writing" a script (with the teacher's help), casting, rehearsing, preparing a stage backdrop, all valuable learning experiences; and to them, most "relevant." The presentation I am told, was a big success, bringing accolades from the principal, pupils, teachers and parents. The principal said he was especially impressed with the performance of the black child who played John Brown, and was considerably nonplussed when Mrs. Smith remarked, with a deliberate touch of irony: "Oh, yes; he has an I.Q. of 80."

More than incidentally, that fourth-grade class's performance in the city wide testing program in the spring was superior to that of any previous fourth-grade class at the school.

There is more than one way to achieve the educational objectives defined in our curriculum bulletins, and a few "Mrs. Smiths" have learned that instructional approaches which link up with the real lives of children always yield the best outcomes. This is especially true in schools serving the poor. The best approach to this subject is found in Mario Fantini's and Gerald Weinstein's discussion of the "relevant curriculum" and "contact classroom methods" in *The Disadvantaged: Challenge to Education*.[1]

Fourth, the almost universal alienation of school from home in the ghetto is still another potent influence toward the non-education of children of the poor. The fact of such alienation hardly requires documentation. A vast gulf of suspicion (and often hostility) generally separates professional staff and parents in poverty areas. In our racially structured society, it is aggravated in neighborhoods where most parents are black and most teachers are white.

If there is anything we can be sure of in education, it is that the school cannot succeed in its efforts without the support of

[1] Mario D. Fantini & Gerald Weinstein, *The Disadvantaged: Challenge to Education* (New York: Harper and Row, 1968).

the home. And I would add as a corollary, it is the professional responsibility of those who man the schools to win such parental support.

Our literature on the disadvantaged is replete with clichés to the effect that impoverished parents are "not interested" in their children's academic progress. This simply is not true. All of the systematic studies I have read support the observations of those who know the poverty community. These studies show that the concerns and aspirations of lower-class parents for their children are strikingly like those of middle-class parents.

True, lower-class parents tend not to visit the school as frequently as middle-class parents, unless they are summoned because their children are failing or causing trouble—and often not even then. Why is this so? Some have young children and cannot afford baby-sitters. Others work during school hours. Many feel uncomfortable when confronted with professionals who are better dressed, more articulate, and confidently "superior" in their manners. And often these parents sense overt racist or social-class prejudices in the office secretary, or even in the principal.

There are several ghetto schools where parents have shown deep concern about their children's education and where there are vital PTAs. In a few schools the staff, and first of all the principal, are genuinely empathetic with their impoverished pupils, and with the parents and the neighborhood as a whole. They "go out of the way" to welcome parents, to involve them in the school's program, and to cope with their problems. Unfortunately, such schools are rare in New York City. Most professional staffs appear to be smugly comfortable in their isolation from the community, or at least unwilling to do anything constructive.

In several in-service courses I have conducted with New York City teachers, I required visits to their pupils' homes— with appointments made in advance. I have always found strong resistance by teachers to the assignment. But they were earning graduate "credits," and had to make the visits. Without exception, they returned enthusiastic. They had been treated with respect and deference, rather than the hostility they feared. More often than not, they were offered food and in some cases drinks. Some of them were walked to the subway by parents after the visits. Almost always they gained important insights into the parents' lives, their problems and hopes, and especially into their children's classroom behavior. As one teacher put it: "I learned more about Helen in that one visit than I could from half a dozen parental visits to the school." Many of them noted improved classroom attitudes and performance by pupils whose homes they visited.

Home visitation is not a common practice among teachers in the ghetto; indeed, in some schools such visits are expressly forbidden. What a pity! There is so much that home visits—and many related professional activities—could do to erode the prevailing alienation of school from home, and thereby to improve the academic behavior of disadvantaged children.

Why do our programs of compensatory education (like most programs in ghetto schools) commonly fail? There is no need for us to seek the answer in pseudo-scientific theories about the "nature" of impoverished children. A stereotyped conception of ghetto children, doubt in their ability to learn, the imposition upon them of prepackaged curricular materials and experiences designed for more affluent children, and the isolation of the schools from the homes and communities from which the pupils come—when these practices prevail among professionals, then the failure of our education programs is readily predictable. And it is necessary that we understand the failure as *ours*, not the children's.

Professional Accountability

The tendency of teachers to disavow responsibility for the noneducation of poor children reflects a characteristic defensiveness. Unlike professionals in other fields, we are not accustomed to being held accountable for results and we resist efforts to appraise our performance on the basis of our pupils' achievement.

We prefer to emphasize our input. Laymen, however, concerned about the life chances of impoverished children, insist on judging the school by its output, by the "product" of the educational enterprise. And I think they are right. Teaching, by definition, is the *guidance of learning*. Where there is no learning, there is no teaching.

The fact that most children from the ghetto may be "harder to teach" than middle-class children (at least by conventional methods) is not a valid excuse for poor performance. If teaching is a profession, not merely a craft, then we must assume responsibility for adapting the methods and materials to the needs of the learners we serve. Just as the physician is judged by whether his patients get well, so must educators be judged by whether their pupils learn.

It is obvious, of course, that many nonschool variables do condition the effectiveness of instruction, and further, that much of our educational technology is still primitive. As professionals, however, we should view this state of affairs as a challenge, not as justification for a "cop out."

Although there is still much to learn about effective approaches to educating these children, several things have been clearly demonstrated. We must stop stereotyping disadvantaged children, and begin to perceive them as the varied individual human beings they are. Professional staffs must be re-educated to understand, and really believe, that children from impoverished backgrounds can learn effectively, and that they do so when guided in appropriate learning experiences. We must stop trying to help disadvantaged children by giving them more and bigger doses of irrelevant curricular materials and methods, and undertake instead a radical revision of the curriculum for the purpose of offering pertinent school experiences. And we must seek and win the cooperation of the home.

How to accomplish these things is the real problem, and I wish I knew the answer. Individual teachers, of course, can read and study and try new methods and materials in their classrooms—which many are doing, but a broader approach is needed to help the thousands of disadvantaged children now being crippled by the schools of New York City. Schools of education could help by supplanting stale programs with more innovative approaches to preparing teachers for the real world. This would not alleviate the problems of teachers in service, whose need for re-education is critical. Those principals who are true educators could do much to further the professional development of their faculties. However, most principals seem to be preoccupied with the "nuts-and-bolts" of administration. I once hoped and believed that the United Federation of Teachers, having attended to problems of teacher welfare, would turn its energies toward upgrading teacher performance. This has proved to be an illusion.

Of course, the primary responsibility for effecting progressive change lies with the Board of Education and its staff of administrators and supervisors, but the resistance of our unparalleled educational bureaucracy to substantial change is notorious. I still have hopes in the burgeoning movement for "community control" of local schools. Once educators are made accountable to the parents whose children we are responsible for educating, I am certain that more effective programs will be developed and implemented.

Dramatic population changes, the onrush of technology, far-reaching developments in our political life, and especially the new forward thrust of the Negro people and other minority groups—all press imperatively for radical changes in public education which the futile gestures of compensatory education cannot satisfy. Our schools have been too slow to adapt to the critical needs of these recent urban developments, but their lag will not be tolerated indefinitely.

I hope our profession is capable of facing up to its responsibility. If not, the forces in the real world around us will intervene effectively.

3

Delinquents and Dropouts:
Some Implications for Schools

WILLIAM C. KVARACEUS

Of the twenty-six million young people who will have entered the business world in this decade, ending in 1970, 25 percent will not have completed high school. One in every nine children will have been referred to a juvenile court for an act of delinquency before his (or her) eighteenth birthday. (For boys, alone, the ratio will be one in every six.) Both statistics are evidence of strong self-destructive tendencies among our youth. In a "credential society" (that is, one which measures individuals by their academic and social achievements) both the dropout and the delinquent move in the direction of social and economic suicide. When these two symptoms combine in one person, he stands in double jeopardy.

The reasons for the academic failure of the socially and emotionally maladjusted, the employed and unemployable, and the delinquent represent areas of the American scene. We need not start from scratch. The research literature is rich with implications for intervention. Building on what we know, I will focus on the need to reshape the school as a social system —a social system that will be an ego-supporting rather than an ego-destroying system.

There is mounting evidence in both dropout and delinquency studies that many provocative and causative factors embedded in these phenomena are school-centered and school-based. The school experiences of the delinquent youngster, as reported in the controlled studies, are generally negative. His report card shows many failures; he is overage for his grade; his attitudes toward school are negative and heavily charged with hate; and he changes schools frequently. He is caught and trapped in the confines of a book-centered curriculum for which he has little preparation and less interest, with the result that he is very difficult to motivate. He intends to leave school as soon as the law will allow, or sooner; and he is frequently truant from his unsatisfactory, frustrating, and degrading school situation. While he represents a severe headache to the school, the school represents an even greater headache to him.

Failure in school, dropping out of school, and delinquency are highly correlated. Kenneth Polk and Lynn Richmond [1] have reported that C and D students in both working- and middle-class families are seven times more likely to be delinquent than A and B students from similar backgrounds. Boys from blue-collar families who failed in school were found to be delinquent almost seven times more often than those who did not fail. In an earlier study in Passaic,[2] I noted an annual fall-off in the number of children referred for norm violation during the summer months when schools were not in session, and when youngsters had more "free time on the streets." Even

[1] Kenneth Polk and Lynn Richmond, "Those Who Fail" (Unpublished paper), Lane County Youth Projects; Eugene, Oregon, 1966.

[2] William C. Kvaraceus, *Juvenile Delinquency and the School* (New York: World Book Co., 1945), p. 152.

with the school referrals factored out (truancy, for example) the drop-off in numbers is still significant. The question—Do some school systems cause delinquency?—must be raised.

The characteristics of dropouts and delinquents, summarized in Tables 3–1 and 3–2, present very similar group profiles and reinforce the notion that we are frequently talking about the same group of youngsters. The composite pictures spell out familiar and common syndromes: history of school failure, dislike for school and school subjects, unsatisfactory student-teacher relationships, a feeling of not belonging, nonparticipation in school activities, and parents of low socioeconomic status. Although intelligence and socioeconomic status have considerable bearing on the problem, recent studies stress inadequate curricula and unsatisfactory relationships between students and school staff as major factors. The emphasis of educational factors within both groups suggests that delinquent- and dropout-prone youths often have school-based roots.

Without minimizing the fact that many noneducational forces are at work in home and community, here I will attempt to explore more fully the interplay of factors affecting the dropout and the delinquent within the structure of the school as a social system that produces both. Leaving school and engaging in norm-violating behavior can be partially explained by psychological or personality traits. But, more often, they are produced by social conditions. To eliminate or at least reduce the dropout rates and delinquent behavior, we must direct our efforts to these social conditions.

In this context Richard Cloward and Lloyd Ohlin made the following observation in the conclusion of their study, *Delinquency and Opportunity*:

We hope that we have at least made it clear that services extending to delinquent individuals or groups cannot prevent the rise of delinquency among others. For delinquency is not, in the final analysis, a property of individuals or even of subcultures; it is a property of the social systems in which these individuals and

Table 3–1 *Common factors Appearing among Potential and Actual Dropouts as Reported by Cervantes*[1]

Two years behind in reading or arithmetic at seventh-grade level. Majority of grades are below average.

Failure of one or more school years (1st, 2nd, 8th, 9th grades most commonly failed; 85 percent of dropouts behind one year; 53 percent two or more years).

Irregular attendance and frequent tardiness. Ill-defined sickness given as reason.

Performance consistently below potential.

No participation in extracurricular activities.

Frequent change of schools.

Behavior problems requiring disciplinary measures.

Feeling of "not belonging" (because of size, speech, personality development, nationality, social class, family disgrace, retardation in school, dress, lack of friends among schoolmates or staff, etc.).

More children than parents can readily control (e.g., only child for divorced and working mother; five or more for nondivorced and working mother of blue- and lower white-collar class).

Parents inconsistent in affection and discipline.

Unhappy family situation (common acceptance, communication, and pleasurable experiences lacking; family solidarity minimal).

Father weak or absent.

Education of parents at eighth-grade level.

Few family friends; among these few many problem units (divorced, deserted, delinquents, dropouts).

Friends not approved by parents.

Friends not school oriented.

Friends much older or much younger.

Resentful of all authority (home, school, police, job, church).

Deferred gratification pattern weak.

Weak self-image.

[1] Lucius F. Cervantes, S.J., *The Dropout: Causes and Cures* (Ann Arbor: University of Michigan Press, 1965).

groups are enmeshed. The pressures that produce delinquency originate in these structures, as do the forces that shape the content of specialized subcultural adaptations. The target for preventive action, then, should be defined, not as the individual or group that exhibits the delinquent pattern, but as the social setting that gives rise to delinquency.[3]

In this vein, I shall discuss the behavioral patterns of the child in the context of the requirements (often impossible) and expectations (sometimes too high but, more frequently, too low) of the school—the school viewed as a particular social system on which depends his acceptance and support as a competent student or his rejection and labeling as retarded, emotionally disturbed, predelinquent, or maladjusted. When there is little tolerance for discrepancy between the behavior of the child and the normal expectancy of the school system, the protest within the system is loud and accommodations are made. This usually takes the form of diagnostic labeling, followed by placing the child in a special class outside the main stream of the system, providing home instruction, suspending or expelling him, or finally carting him off to a special school or institution. The system, thus, succeeds in placating the noise makers until the next complaint, and then the process is repeated.

Some Structures in the Social System of the School

All schools face certain persistent problems. The problems of the learner are his serious lack of motivation, academic failure, truancy, early school leaving, disruptive behavior in the classroom, delinquent behavior on the playground, and vandalism. On the other hand, the teacher frequently resists change, is hostile toward the administration, and forms unproductive relationships with colleagues and students. To prevent or to

[3] Richard A. Cloward and Lloyd E. Ohlin, *Delinquency and Opportunity* (New York: Free Press, 1960), p. 211.

TABLE 3-2 *Personal and Environmental Deviations of Many Delinquents as Reported in Controlled Studies of Delinquents and Nondelinquents (After Kvaraceus[1])*

DEVIATIONS IN PERSONAL MAKE-UP	DEVIATIONS IN HOME, FAMILY AND NEIGHBORHOOD	DEVIATIONS IN SCHOOL
Mean IQ—89 (Lower academic aptitude or verbal intelligence requiring abstraction, concentration, persistence)	Contradictory social norms in home and/or neighborhood	"Poor" or failure marks
Mesomorphic (muscular) constitution	Identified with delinquent subculture	Repeater (retarded in grade)
Emotional malfunctioning and disturbances	Atypical home structure (broken home)	Strong dislike and hostility for school
Superego—delinquency identified; value system not internalized	Interpersonal relationships in home wanting	Truancy
Assertiveness strong	Economic stress, insecurity and/or substandard economic conditions	Intent to leave school early
Defiance high		Vague or no educational goals
Resentfulness high	Lack of moral conformity—spiritual values lacking; little or nominal church contact	Motivational problem
Ambivalent attitude toward authority		Member of special class
Impulsiveness	Criminality pattern	Has attended many different schools
High anxiety pattern	Culture conflicts	Destroys school material and property
High hostility and resentment	Deteriorated neighborhood residence	Does not feel he "belongs" in classroom
Strong distrust toward authority	Discipline overstrict, punitive, erratic, lax	Does not participate in volunteer extracurricular school activities
Aggression—overt and retaliatory	Lack of cohesiveness	Serious and persistently misbehaving in school
Unsocialized aggression	Supervision by mother inadequate or unsuitable	
Emotional lability and/or impulsiveness	Affection of parents indifferent or hostile	
Egocentricism and self-indulgence		
Suggestibility strong		
Low frustration-tolerance		
Adventurous spirit		
Moral psychopathic tendency		
Hypomanic tendency strong		
Low neurotic pattern		

[1] William C. Kvaraceus, *Community and the Delinquent* (New York: World Book Co., 1966), pp. 85–109.

solve these problems school officials frequently turn to the ancillary services offered by the counselor, school psychologist, social worker, or psychiatrist. Frequently, these services fail to relieve or remediate the problem. One reason for this failure is the fact that the problem is the product of forces rooted not in the psyche or in the family but, rather, in the social system of the school. School personnel need to be aware of those aspects of the system that give rise to various problems, in part or wholly, because of the social habitat in which teachers and pupils live and work.

In the bureaucracy of the school, there is a vast network of interpersonal relationships that impinge on problems of learning, behavior, administration, and emotional climate. The success of any new program, regardless of its intrinsic merit, will depend on forces in the social system of the school as much as on the plan itself. Why is it that innovation and change are never easy in the business of the school? There are a number of dimensions in the social system that can help to answer this question.

The *formal work structure* in the school provides an unwritten job description of role expectancy. The introduction of classroom aides, paraprofessionals, teaching teams, and programmed instruction can be upsetting to the teacher unless he understands what the role of the aide, colleague, or teaching machine is and how this affects his own teaching role. Classroom aides can threaten the teacher who generally suffers from an overly slick professionalism, supported by the master's degree from State University. The wide and successful use of student tutors and classroom aides provides sufficient evidence that "untrained" teachers can also teach. The new workers, as well as the old workers, need to know their exact job-role. The teacher will have to relinquish certain tools and tasks to his assistants and to share many others, in order to organize his duties into manageable units. With two or three willing aides, the teacher could hopefully manage the teaching tasks.

There is a great deal of confusion in the school today regarding the *authority structure* and the *power structure*. Decision making is an essential component of authority structure. The person who signs the requisition slips has the authority. There is also, however, the power to influence. The teachers in the department can vote and petition authority to purchase certain texts or to change the sequence or content of courses. A faculty member may prefer to join the AFT rather than the NEA, believing one has more influence or power than the other. Teachers today have more power than ever before. Negotiations between teacher associations and school boards involve everything from school discipline to salaries.

What power does the student have to influence change when he is caught in an inefficient, irrelevant, and boring school situation? What power do his parents have to improve the school system and to change harmful school practices? It may be necessary to include both parents and students so that they can deal with the corporate structure of the school board or board of trustees. The current movement in the big cities to include parents and the indigenous neighborhood leadership in planning, administering, and evaluating programs in school and community reflects this concern. The Black Power concept, in which the intent to gain influence is intrinsic, is partly responsible for this demand for community involvement.

In slow-moving, slow-changing schools, it may be the students themselves who will eventually constitute the only leverage to influence official authority to re-evaluate the school and the classroom and to move more quickly toward improving the learning conditions. In fact, this is now the situation on many college campuses; it will soon start extending to the high schools, as has the use of caps and gowns, the "bowl football games," and the fraternity system.

The *structure of status and prestige* in the social system of the school serves as another important dimension for both faculty and students. In some high schools, girls would rather be popular and boys would prefer to be football heroes rather than students and scholars. How a student achieves esteem and acclaim will explain the motivation of many students. To be accepted for admission by an Ivy League school may give a student high status in one school; while the student who returns from Juvenile Court after having received his credentials as an adjudicated delinquent may be equally honored in another school system. There are some subjects (and, therefore, teachers) and courses that carry more status and prestige than others. Every school has its special dumping ground. Claude Brown's comment hints at this situation.

I was having a rough time in school. I was taking an academic course, and the only thing that I knew anything about was English, and I only knew a little bit about that. Geometry and algebra were kicking my ass. When I was going to high school during the day, I told them I wanted to take an academic course, but they said I couldn't take that because my math wasn't strong enough. They put me in a commercial course.[4]

Sometimes a student is placed in a special class or even a "general course"; which serves to label the student and to prescribe his actions. School is more than an educational agency—it is a social system, and a classifying agent; and it can "hound" and trap students, who are powerless to defend themselves. Educators must involve youth in school decision making, and thus enpower them to study and to solve their educational problems. Everything that concerns the pupil should be negotiable, just as everything that concerns the teacher is now negotiable.

The lines of *communication* in the social system of the school are usually clogged. The switchboard is overburdened with callers, and the lines are busy. Few pupils bother to pick up the receiver. People may seem to listen, but no one really hears the other. It is not easy for a middle-class, white, female teacher

4 Claude Brown, *Manchild in the Promised Land* (New York: The Macmillan Co., 1965), p. 179.

to communicate with a poor white or black or Puerto Rican pupil. Sometimes a gesture can breach the barriers more easily than words, as Claude Brown points out in *Manchild in the Promised Land.*

One day, Mrs. Cohen gave me a book. It was an autobiography of some woman by the name of Mary McLeod Bethune. When she gave it to me, she said, "Here's something you might like to read." Before that, I had just read pocketbooks. I'd stopped reading comic books, but I was reading the trashy pocketbooks, stuff like *Duke, The Golden Spike,* that kind of nonsense.

I just took it and said, "Yeah, uh-huh." I saw the title on it, but I didn't know who the woman was. I just took it because Mrs. Cohen had given it to me. I said, "Yeah, I'll read it," and I read it because I figured she might ask about it, and I'd have to know something. It wasn't too bad. I felt that I knew something; I knew who Mary McLeod Bethune was, and I figured I probably knew as much about her as anybody else who knew anything about her, after reading a book about her whole life. Anyway, I felt a little smarter afterward.[5]

The nonverbal clues in communicating with advantaged as well as disadvantaged youngsters in the classroom are more telling than the words that are used. Who believes anyone outside the youth camp these days? Video tapes from inner-city classrooms indicate that teacher's smiles, raised eyebrows, frowns, body position, and gestures are an important aspect of the communication process. At times, they are better media then words, and often they belie the word.

Last, the *informal and clique-group structure* of the school, whether seen in the huddle of teachers in the faculty room rehashing the latest memorandum from the principal's office or in the small knot of pupils griping about their marks in the corner drugstore, plays an important part in the collective and private school life of students and teachers. It is in these intimate groups that youngsters express their fears and anxieties, their hopes and expectations. Somehow, these need to be

[5] *Ibid.,* p. 156.

tapped and used to advantage in improving the climate and the way of life in the social system.

Some Implications and Contingencies for Schools [6]

The temptation to make the school an omnibus agency to serve any community endeavor is always present. The school, as one agency, cannot hope to be everything to every child. The school is not a hospital or a clinic. It is not a community warehouse for disturbed or disturbing children and youth; nor is it an adolescent ghetto or limbo. The unique and special role of the school is to be found in its teaching-learning function aimed at specific objectives.

Keeping in focus this unique and special function, and recognizing the fact that most of the delinquents' difficulties stem from forces and antecedents outside the school, just what can be expected of the school staff in community programs aimed at keeping children in school and curbing delinquency? What is the potential role of the classroom teacher, the school administrator, and the school counselor?

Our chances for reducing school dropouts and delinquent behavior will depend upon our focus on the school as a social system and on the extent to which we meet certain basic conditions or contingencies.

The schools must break through the age barriers. The critical social issue of the past twenty years has centered around vertical mobility and the opportunity to improve one's socio-economic status. This issue has now come to a head and hopefully will be resolved at last. The critical social issue of the next fifty years will turn around old children and childish adults'

[6] Portions of the following have been summarized from William C. Kvaraceus, *Anxious Youth: Dynamics of Delinquency* (Columbus, Ohio: Charles Merrill Books, Inc., 1966) and "Delinquency Prevention: Legislation, Financing, and Law Enforcement Are Not Enough," *Crime and Delinquency* (October, 1969), 463–470.

relationships. Already the enemy camps are being staked out in a we-and-they struggle.

If we study the age line from birth to death, we can readily identify certain distinct age groupings. First, we have the preschool group which is the object of much public and private concern recognizing the importance of the first five years of life. Head Start Programs, for example, testify, and rightfully so, to our concern for this age group and their future welfare. This is the "vaccination card-carrying crowd." Next, are those youngsters sitting in the classrooms or the "report-card crowd." (Can you imagine one of your students burning his report card on the steps of your high school building?) Then, there is the "draft-card cluster," following in the steps of the "social security card group" who will soon join the "medicare card-carrying members." A situation in which youth no longer trusts those over the age of twenty-nine (or is it now twenty-six?) indicates something more than a generation gap. Two opposing forces are developing, with only limited communication between them. It is difficult to assess, for example, how much of the youthful crime (peaking at age fifteen and cresting on the school leaving line of sixteen), and how much of the rioting among the youth is attributable to the "we-them" feeling of hostility between youth and adults and how much is attributable to other forces in family, neighborhood, and school. Since schools are run by adults with captive youth, they represent a pressure cooker that is now beginning to blow in many schools, although most schools have ways of removing the more recalcitrant pupils.

The schools must provide a positive, therapeutic, and reconstructive climate for the nonachieving and misbehaving child. There are four mood orientations that can be found in varying degree in every school and community. They include: the punitive-retaliatory mood, the positive-humanistic mood, the therapeutic mood, and the cultural-reconstructionive mood.

The *punitive-retaliatory* orientation is the dominant mood in most schools and communities today. The man-in-the-street, many classroom teachers, and some professional workers with youths and families want to deal with the delinquent by striking back at him and his parents. This is the "get tough" and "treat them rough" school of thought. It includes all those who advocate greater use of the paddle or night stick, curfew, and suspension and exclusion from school. The underlying theme is that the young offender (and his parents) should not be tolerated. Rather, they should be made to suffer. And having suffered, the delinquent is expected to have learned a lesson that he is not to violate any norms again. Illustrations of the strength of this mood can be found in the recent NEA reports studying working conditions of teachers. The second greatest problem cited by teachers concerned the reluctant and recalcitrant learner. (The greatest problem was over-large class size.) Forty-five percent of the teachers urged that some provision be made outside the regular classroom for these disturbed or disturbing nonlearners, and 48 percent of the principals endorsed this move. Even the Conant report on the American High School[7] subtly, if not wisely, urged that these youngsters might be eased out of school at the age of fourteen, if they could not or would not learn.

The *positive-humanistic mood* is also visible in many schools and classrooms. This orientation considers the delinquent, not so much a problem child, as a child with a problem. The conviction is expressed that there are causes or reasons for the norm violation and that the delinquent is in need of a helping hand, rather than the back of the hand. But the school-community effort generally responds to the delinquency problem via the media of a new playground, an essay contest, or the appointment of a kindly old assistant principal to work with young boys and girls who get in trouble.

[7] James B. Conant, *The American High School Today* (New York: McGraw-Hill Book Co., 1959).

The dominant orientation among professional workers in dealing with the delinquents and their families is evident in the *therapeutic mood*. Here the underlying premise is that the youthful offender suffers interpsychic conflicts stemming largely from forces under the skin and/or interpersonal relationships in the family. The plea is made to procure adequate psychological, psychiatric, and case-work services. An answer soon shapes up in the form of the child guidance center. The conviction is that the delinquent is sick and he is to be treated as a patient.

The fourth orientation, only recently seen in a few of the larger urban centers, can be described as the *cultural-reconstruction mood*. This approach assumes that the basic problem in many—if not most—delinquency cases involves values and value systems. The cultural and subcultural determinants of behavior are studied, and the norm violator is viewed as reacting to the demands and the standards set up within his primary reference group as found in the family, gang, neighborhood, school, and community. Within this approach, it is the youngster's essential and intimate reference group that is viewed as the patient. Concern is expressed for the child's rule book as found in his milieu. Community forces—home, church, school, club—regard themselves as "change agents." This approach, only now making itself felt, promises a much needed supplement to the more traditional school-community efforts.

Today many schools caught in the press of the educational critics demanding more and better mathematicians, scientists, and linguists appear more than willing to sell any misbehaving nonlearner down the river to preserve the academic reputation of the school. Little hope or help can be forthcoming from schools that are devoid of redemptive love, that fail to provide a therapeutic climate, and that have little or no effect on the behavior or way of life of those it is committed to change through the educational growth process.

School programs can provide the understanding, enabling,

and therapeutic climate for those youngsters who are bothered or bothersome, but they should do so without dropping their true educational function or without specializing their educational program as to downgrade the student by placing a low ceiling on his potential and thus truncating his career line. I shall return to this concern again.

The teacher must be authentic and play his teaching role effectively in the classroom. Both the study of equality in education made by the United States Office of Education,[8] and the evaluation by the National Advisory Council on the Education of Disadvantaged Children of Title I projects of the ESE Act of 1965 offer evidence that the competency of the teacher and the quality of relationship—the rapport between teacher and child—are crucial to the improvement of service to the disadvantaged.

The teacher's essential role and function is not therapeutic; it is not to brainwash or to indoctrinate to middle-class values. The unique and essential feature of the teacher's role is to educate—to develop the cognitive processes. The school is not a hospital or a jail; nor is it a warehouse in which to store young people or a social or recreational agency. The school is a unique opportunity to learn and to develop rational thinking. In this role, the teacher functions by motivating children, by guiding the learning activities toward selected objectives, and by evaluating the product and the process of learning. But the teacher cannot carry out these functions unless he is *authentic*. There are three aspects of authenticity that a teacher must possess that are crucial for all especially when he is dealing with the underachievers, potential dropouts and delinquents.

First, substantively the teacher must be knowledgeable or expert in his field. Teachers of history must know history;

[8] James S. Coleman, et al., *Equality of Educational Opportunity* (Washington, D.C.: U.S. Government Printing Office, 1966).

teachers of science must be versed in science; teachers of mathematics must be mathematicians. Working recently in the public school system of a large eastern city, I heard the local school authorities complain frequently that they were facing a serious teacher shortage and that they had "1200 vacancies." I asked, "Do you really have 1200 uncovered classrooms?" They answered, "Of course not, but we do have 1200 marginal teachers." How does it feel to be a marginal teacher and how does it feel to have a marginal teacher? Marginal mentors, poorly equipped for teaching in a given field, exude an insecurity that is contagious. Uncertain teachers run the risk of producing uncertain students. It is questionable that third-rate teachers can produce first-rate scholars. Students—white or black—know when a teacher has mastered his subject matter. They are sensitive to expertise and scholarship and resent the insecure and the make-believe scholars.

Second, the teacher himself must serve as the symbol and the embodiment of his goals and his subject matter. There are teachers of English who invite their class to enjoy their first experience in reading *Julius Caeser* or in reading lyric verse, but who had to be forced to include these courses as a part of their "major" in college. Most of these teachers have long ago sold their college English texts to the secondhand bookstore, and they have not bought or read a Shakespearean play or a lyric verse since. The intellectual model is a rarity in the American high school. It is not necessary to look at the range of test scores in teacher-preparation institutions and departments of education to verify this. (These are available for those who require such data.) It is sufficient to inspect the intellectual behavior and reading habits of secondary school teachers who seldom exemplify the goals they are trying to sell in their classes. Recent studies [9] by the NEA confirm that the

[9] W. A. Graves, "Teachers' Reading and Recreational Interests," *NEA Journal*, November 1966, pp. 17–19.

level of teaching reading is in the zone of the *Reader's Digest*. Yet I have heard a history teacher exclaim, "You know, this year I have two young historians in my classes." When this happens, you can be sure it is because he has been more than a teacher of history. It is because he has been thinking, talking, and acting like an historian.

Third, and most important, as we have pointed out earlier, the teacher must ring true in his interpersonal relationships with his students. There are two kinds of fear dominating inner-city classrooms. Many teachers in deprived areas fear their students, particularly black students. These teachers are also afraid of bright students who challenge them and who find the correct answers via routes other than those promulgated officially by the teacher. The current national trend to place police personnel in secondary schools reflects the basic fear now visible in many American classrooms.

The surrogate role of the teacher must be maximized. Who wants to be like the teacher? Many teachers do, and more could, serve as imitable examples in the old tradition of competency models by developing stronger interpersonal relationships with students. The threat of oversized classrooms, teaching machines, and listless mentors, anonymity, impersonality, and boredom can combine to create the early school dropout. This means that the instructor in the high school program will have to serve as a hero model. But he will not be able to serve in this capacity if he himself feels he has little status or prestige and if he himself suffers from low self-concept.

To summarize: unless the teacher knows his subject matter, unless he lives out the objectives of his course, and unless he establishes a positive relationship based on mutual trust and respect, students will perceive him as a fraud.

School personnel must achieve greater differentiation of curriculum and instruction. A recent study of values held by high school pupils, their teachers, and their parents in five New

England communities found that high school pupils, with very few exceptions, testified to the importance of schooling, as did their teachers and parents; but the same students also reported that there was nothing so boring as school.[10] With the support of their parents and peers, it is possible for most middle-class students to endure any kind of academic nonsense and to survive the rituals and redundancies of the secondary school. Lacking such reinforcement and support, it is the rare Claude Brown who will muster the ego strength and the long-distance vision to endure the high school experience in a slum school of the inner city or the depressed rural community.

A great danger to the student in some newly adopted programs is that the curriculum is so modified and unsubstantial that the youngster spends most of his time with the jig saw making door stops or with reading materials one level above the comic book. Courses that take on a "practical" and "utilitarian" complexion and that prepare the youngsters only for a rote and standardized occupation can be so lacking in the intellectual and ideational area as to degrade and demean a student's self-concept. Unless the new school approaches widen occupational horizons and uplift self-esteem, they will neither educate nor rehabilitate.

In addition to its traditional functions of transmitting heritage and of developing the rational powers, the modern school must view itself as an agency for cultural renewal and change. The objectives of character development, beneficial use of leisure time, vocational training, worthwhile family relationships, and civic and social competency must be placed in proper perspective as we raise the question, "What are we educating for?" The objectives of the school must be re-examined against the needs of all pupils, including the serious norm violators, and the needs of our urbanized and technological society. Here

[10] William C. Kvaraceus, "Working with Youth: Some Operational Principles," *American Journal of Catholic Youth Work* (Spring 1968): 47–53.

is the major challenge to those planning prevention and rehabilitation programs.

Furthermore, school objectives must be stated, and the evaluation of the school's program should be made in terms of the development of new and desirable behavior patterns or of the modification of old, undesirable ones. If schools can modify the behaviors of large groups of children, they may justify their potential as an agent for cultural renewal and change. If schools cannot perform this function, they face the imminent danger of becoming the most expensive irrelevancy of the twentieth century.

The school must be as cognizant of its subliminal or covert curriculum as of the visible courses of study. There are two curricula in every school. There is the overt curriculum, which consists of all those planned activities which are pointed toward agreed-upon objectives. There is also the covert curriculum, hidden in the culture and subcultures of the school; this is the way of life that tells the student how to behave and how not to behave. Like the lower part of the iceberg, it can be a subtle and formidable determinant of educational behavior. The United States Office of Education Study of Equality testified to the importance of this aspect of school life when it reported that pupil achievement was found to be strongly related to the educational backgrounds and aspirations of other students in the school. Many black parents intuitively sense this in their fight against de facto segregation. The imbalance blurs the value system and weakens the motivational forces that support educational activities and objectives. The subliminal curriculum can determine whether a student will gain status and prestige as a truant or as an honor student.

There are many dimensions to be explored in the area of the subliminal curriculum. These may vary from school to school, but whatever the pattern, it is a unique substructure that can support or interfere with the basic tasks of the school.

Coeducational activities, delayed responsibility, the learning style and schedule of "clock and calendar," homogeneous grouping by age and ability, vague and undetermined futuristic goals, the external controls exercised by school staff, the passive activity level prescribed by the school, the compulsory nature of school attendance—all these factors combine to make up the fabric of the covert curriculum.

Early identification of pupils vulnerable or exposed to the development of delinquent behavior can best be carried on in the school agency. While there is no tool, table, or test that can be used to identify the future delinquent, some youngsters give many indications of incipient delinquency and can be readily identified for referral and help.

In a three-year prediction study involving a careful before-after design in grades seven, eight, and nine, which I have reported in *Exceptional Children*,[11] the prediction scales utilized failed to meet the stringent tests of functional and statistical needs incorporated in the research design around the criterion of norm-violating behavior. Nevertheless, this study did indicate that the behavioral observations and ratings of experienced junior high school teachers showed more promise as a method of identifying the future norm violators than did the psychological scales. Few youngsters become delinquent overnight. In the long sequitur of behavior, the alert teacher receives many hints of future difficulties, for "nothing predicts behavior like behavior." By drawing the pre-delinquent into the rehabilitation program early, the vocational specialists may play a preventive role.

This same study also pointed up the fact that junior high school youngsters who fall into the lowest or poorest reading group tend to show a heavy preponderance of norm violations. Reading disability, whether it be cause or effect, must be taken

[11] William C. Kvaraceus, "Forecasting Delinquency: A Three-year Experiment," *Exceptional Children*, 27 (Spring 1961): 429–435.

into account as a potential factor closely tied in with the delinquency and dropout symptoms. Attention to the poorest readers by the schools may enable the community to focus on a group of youngsters who are already, or who will be, showing behavioral disturbances.

Table 3-3 provides promising schemata that can be used to identify vulnerability in the lower- or middle-class youngster. The screening process involves two major steps and takes into account important distinctions between the genesis of lower-class delinquency and middle-class norm violations. The first step involves the identification of class status. The second step uses subindicators to note factors that are frequently associated

TABLE 3-3   *Delinquency Prediction Schemata*

DISCRIMINATION LEVEL I: FOR PRIMARY REFERENCE GROUP
Purpose: to identify child's cultural milieu

Parents do not belong to organized groups like PTA, Women's Club, Elks, Lions, Redmen, Lodges	Parents belong to several organized groups such as PTA, Women's Club, Elks, Lions, Redmen
Female based household	Flavor of female dominated household
School drop out: actual or intentional	Finish high school and intends to go to college
Speech patterns: Utilizes non-school supported grammatical features—e.g. "ain't," "we don't hardly"	Speech patterns: Utilizes school supported grammatical system
Low scholastic performance	High scholastic performance in school
Orientation on "being"	Orientation on "becoming"
Property concern: to use and wear out	Property concern: to maintain and improve
Family spends it and enjoys it now	Family saves and insures for the future
Fate and luck	Plan and system
Male kin are tattooed	Male kin not tattooed
Gets money for personal use: catch as catch can	Is provided a weekly or monthly allowance

Purpose: to select the most vulnerable youngster

Runs with gang wherein prestige and status is geared to law-violating behavior

Shows high level of aspiration without means or opportunity to achieve

Has academic interest and/or performance but runs the gamut of gang's criticism

Uses school as arena for physical skill, force, excitement

Family or gang constantly getting into trouble with authority (school, church, police)

Shows smartness and good conning techniques

Shows "independence" by nonadherence to rules and regulations and by aggressive, overt, attacking behavior

Poor school performance and failure

Withdraws with explosive potential

Household pattern differs from stable nuclear father-mother household

Interpersonal relationships among family members tense and conflicting, repressive and/or overprotective

Intends to leave school early

Far below average for his grade

Truants from school

Low academic aptitude

Shows heavy guilt involvement

Inadequate identification with appropriate parent figure

Shows consistent patterning of norm-violating acts along the dimensions of concerns of lower-class society

Social isolation from gang

Heavy pressure from friends and family against continuing in school

Finds excitement in vandalism, collective stealing

Reacts aggressively to conflicts between norms of home and values of school and society

Living in accordance with petty crime climate condoning law violations

Fights his problems out

Registers overt defiance toward authority

Takes it out on people and property

Identifies with female authority figure

Lacks appropriate father figure

History of enuresis (bed-wetting), tics, nail-biting, persistent sleep disturbances

Passive and overdependent

Characteristically anxious

Suspicious—fears the worst in a passive rather than in a belligerent manner

Ego weak—superego of inhibitors strong

PREDELINQUENT: NEEDING SECOND LOOK AND HELPING HAND

Reprinted from William C. Kvaraceus, *Anxious Youth: Dynamics of Delinquency* (Columbus, Ohio: Charles Merrill Books, Inc., 1966) pp. 112–113. Reprinted by permission of Charles E. Merrill Publishing Company.

with conflicts and frustrations which generate norm- and rule-violating behavior within each milieu.

For those youngsters who manifest learning difficulties and symptoms of emotional disturbance, the school must procure and maintain certain special and essential services. The teacher's time and competencies are limited. He needs the help of the school nurse, school doctor, counselor, psychologist, case worker. To the usual array of services, we need to add those of a social analyst. Drawn from the disciplines of sociology and cultural anthropology, this functionary would aim to help school personnel to understand the society of the school and the cultural and subcultural currents within the school and the community. This social scientist would be concerned primarily with the dynamics of behavior as found in the individual's milieu. This worker would serve as a complement to the psychologists or guidance workers who tend to concern themselves almost exclusively with psychic determinants of behavior.

The school administration must provide therapeutic resources and counseling aids for the staff. Teachers are persons and, like their pupils, they also have problems and frequently need help. When a problem-laden teacher meets a troubled pupil, a clash is inevitable. Teaching a large class of different and often difficult pupils day in and day out makes unusual demands on a teacher's personality. When the going gets rough, teachers need ready access to an accepting and understanding administrator or counselor to whom they can gripe, beef, remonstrate, and unload. If relationships with the staff are positive and of a nonjudgmental nature, these functionaries should be able to play the therapeutic-listening role of the good administrator or supervisor. In this way, the principal's office can become a comfortable listening post or haven for the overworked, hard-pressed, harassed, and unhappy teacher. This is the easiest form of counseling and one that can do the least damage. If no one on the teaching staff ever comes by to discuss his problems with the administrator or supervisor on his own initiative, it is probably the administrator who needs help.

The school must improve its partnership role within the total community complex of health and welfare agencies. The school cannot remain an isolated agency. It must coordinate its efforts with those of other youth, family, welfare and recreation agencies. There are many covert conflicts in school and community that drain off the administrators' and teachers' energies which would be better applied to helping the norm-violating youngsters. Many of these conflicts can be found along the following bipolar dimensions: action vs. theory, rehabilitation vs. retaliation, centralization of services vs. localization of services, subjectivity vs. objectivity, student activity vs. student passivity. Lack of any real coordination or teamwork can frequently be attributed to these subliminal conflict issues.

Summary

In mobilizing community forces for prevention and control of juvenile delinquency, the social planner intuitively looks to the school as a major—if not central—resource. The schools have all the children of all the people; they receive the child at an early age and maintain a close and intimate relationship with him for an extended period of time; they have trained personnel to deal with children and youth; they strive to develop integrated and socially effective citizens; they are found in every community; and they still enjoy the active support of the community at large. Without the school's active support, the community will not have much effect on its delinquency and dropout problems. But the school, acting in concert with all community agencies and resources, can do much to reduce the twin problems that threaten a large segment of the nation's youth.

4

New Methods of Teaching the Socially Disadvantaged

ROBERT A. DENTLER

Before discussing the new trends in educating so-called disadvantaged students, I will sketch briefly why this is the subject of concern. What priority would we ascribe to this problem to indicate its importance? Where have educators indicated their concern—aside from the usual academic lip service employed in every introductory survey course, in every college program in the fall? As most people are well aware, both from experience and from the media, urban poverty, welfare dependency and race or ethnicity are intertwined. Daniel P. Moynihan gave this particular combination of dilemmas first priority in his recent and exhaustive analysis of national policy toward urban problems. Dr. Moynihan said:

The poverty and social isolation of minority groups in central cities is the single, most serious problem of the American city today. It must be attacked with urgency, with a greater commitment of resources than has heretofore been the case, and with programs designed especially for this purpose.[1]

At the Center for Urban Education we agree with Dr. Moynihan's judgment that the first line of attack on this bilateral problem of poverty and the isolation of minority groups in central cities should be the immediate federal reform of the welfare system. It is just coincidental that this particular plea was made by the President of the United States. We agree, too, that the second line of attack upon this problem should be to enact policies that would foster work and the opportunity to earn an adequate income for adults and young adults of inner-city minorities.

The third and most deeply preventive approach to the problem should be the strategic reconstruction of urban education. It is this priority with which I shall concern myself in this article. As reported in the most authoritative economic analysis of poverty, *Income and Welfare in the United States*, "Above all since education has proven to be the crucial nexis in intergenerational change, the long run elimination of welfare dependency hinges most upon reducing the dropouts and increasing the quality of education."[2] What the author James Morgan and his associates at the University of Michigan mean by this conclusion is that the cycle of poverty and the cycle of welfare dependency both embrace more than one family generation. If the two cycles are to be broken with some degree of permanence, it must be done by upgrading the earning power and cognitive skills of the child within the impoverished family.

Other approaches that I would utilize would be to reform the welfare system itself and establish a new order of economic

---

[1] Daniel P. Moynihan, ed., *Toward a National Urban Policy* (New York: Basic Books, Inc., 1970), p. 9.

[2] James Morgan, et al., *Income and Welfare in the United States* (New York: McGraw-Hill, 1962), p. 11.

growth. But the cycles of poverty and dependency cannot be broken by the upcoming generation without more effective educational intervention. It is my belief that this educational intervention is not now taking place in our city school systems, public or private, on a meaningful scale. The Governor's Commission on the Los Angeles riots stated that present educational programs in the cities are not intensive enough to make the major change in academic achievement that is crucial. Unless a large majority of students in disadvantaged neighborhoods learn to read and write before they enter the fifth grade, no matter what the cost, the war against poverty will be lost.

We have just completed at CUE, under commission from the Secretary of Health, Education and Welfare and the Commissioner of Education a series of ten memoranda considering the nature of the problem and recommending a number of federal approaches to its solution. We have compiled evidence from thirteen of the largest cities in the country and have made comparisons between these and their suburban, white, affluent counterparts which have lead us to the above judgments.

At the present time, big city school systems are unable to intervene effectively in three rather obvious ways. First, the efforts of the systems at compensatory education at the pre-school level have been unsuccessful thus far. Second, welfare-linked school services, such as school social workers, are pitifully inadequate in the largest cities and nonexistent in the smaller ones. Third, city schools have not yet closed the gap on sheer formal educational attainment. In spite of intriguing and promising improvements between 1960 and 1968 in this respect, the urban dropout rate as a whole continues to exceed 27 percent and to reach 39 percent among the ghetto poor. So I would not give first priority to a careful consideration of the ways in which the problem of poverty and oppression might be resolved by changes in urban education. I refuse to pretend that this is the country's *most* pressing challenge, but I will settle for and be willing to argue about third place, which still makes it most worthy of our attention.

Let us consider, before we get into the positive aspects of this topic, the term "disadvantaged." There are now nearly a thousand entries in ERIC, the government's information retrieval system on education, on the subject of the educationally disadvantaged. I shall not take you through this literature. I have in mind, instead, a peculiar definition which is grounded in the experiences over the last four years at the Center for Urban Education and the center's collaboration with a number of college and university teams in New York City. First of all, note that the word "disadvantaged" reflects Western and, particularly, the American free-enterprise culture. Disadvantaged is a "game" term. It implies a competitive relationship. In a game such as tennis there is no score that is made by being "disadvantaged." On the point after you secure the "advantage," you secure the game.

In short, disadvantaged is simply a statement about social competition. In terms of its origin in the behavioral sciences and educational research circles, it is a cover term; a label which releases us from having to say "Low SES" or "Low I.Q." In a free-enterprise culture, we have many persons of low SES and low I.Q. who compete beautifully and who are therefore obviously *advantaged*. SES is the sociologist's equivalent of I.Q. It refers to socioeconomic status. But it is socially unacceptable to discuss a person's intelligence or social class. Besides, it would lead to misjudgments, since neither of these two factors (which are the ones we can measure somewhat in the behavioral sciences) is pertinent to the subject of learning. Neither can reliably guarantee the degree of competitive success an individual will have; and it is competitive success that underlies the concept of advantaged. To label a person disadvantaged is to imply he will have trouble "making it" (whatever that is). This is not a psychological term, although a glance at the literature will show that educational and clinical psychologists have at government expense, embellished the term with clinical properties.

As a student of this literature, I can find no personality attributes that might be reliably or validly associated with the concept. Therefore, I think it is a social term which explains one person's prospects vis-à-vis other persons' prospects. My definition hinges on this recognition of the "game" properties, the competitive underpinning of the term "disadvantaged."

From this point of view, the disadvantaged student is one who is least likely, before he undergoes instruction, to have mastered learning skills. The disadvantaged student is the least equipped to compensate for poor instruction during the instructional process. Also, the disadvantaged student is one who is least able to exploit his apparent educational attainments after completing study.

While this is a simple conceptual cloak upon which to clothe my subject, it also represents something about teaching and learning. Teaching and learning really occur and reoccur throughout one's existence on a before, during, and after basis. I am hopelessly locked in the pre-McLuhan era when stories tended to have a beginning, middle, and end. I shall trace the remainder of my treatment of new approaches in terms of this before, during, and after.

Let me state that "before" is not a prenatal or a preschool state. "During" is not kindergarten through twelve, nor is "after," a state that happens when you depart from adolescence at age thirty. Before, during, and after are phenomena that are repeated over and over again as one enters and exits from a teaching-learning situation.

I wish to discuss the "before" category first. I have said that the disadvantaged student is the one who is least likely, prior to instruction, to already have mastered the subject. If you look at our "advantaged" school systems from Harvard and the Ivy League down to the humblest school, you will recognize that our advantaged system presupposes that the student has mastered most of the skills of the subject area on entry into school. My experience in the rich, old-time prep schools of New England where I have both taught and done research on student behavior, and my experience as a professor at Dartmouth, Columbia, and Cornell, convince me that the student in these schools is *expected* to be competent on arrival. Whatever competencies he lacks result in low grades and a more trying initial adjustment period.

Examining the skills of students in elite schools, we find that the first-grade child may already read at the fourth-grade level according to national norms. Each year in a school sequence for the advantaged child is a social pleasure. Having already mastered the basic skills and most of the subject areas, students can have a good time wrestling and rustling about in the particulars and rehearsing and reliving feelings of mastery. A sociologist colleague of mine, after his first year of teaching Yale undergraduates said, "I'll have to leave. There is nothing that can be taught." The Yale student often assumes that because he has been admitted, he must already be knowledgeable enough to graduate—and the student's assessment is roughly correct.

In the disadvantaged instance, we are aware that the child does *not* arrive in a state of prior mastery. Whatever else he has going for him—cunning, hope, good will—he does not have advanced mastery. Indeed, he naively assumes that is what he came to school to secure. Research, as reported in the much doubted Westinghouse Head Start evaluation which indicates the noneffect (comparatively speaking) of the nation's Head Start programs over the last two years, gives rise to the implication that: *the preschool programs that operate under the banner of Head Start are faulty because they are the wrong kinds of programs.* In other words, for all the valiant and critically important undertakings that are involved in shifting resources, it is still true that teachers and teacher aides are not able to cope with the "before" state in a child. In short, we think the program that is missing is the program which would structure not the child's but the teacher's behavior. This is the definition of an instructional program that copes with the "before" state of educational disadvantage.

If the child is to have less of a disadvantage, we must be very definite about the programs that will make this a reality. One of our greatest joys at the Center for Urban Education has been the pursuit over the last four years of a preschool project we call the "C.H.I.L.D. Project," under the leadership of Professor Helen Robison at Teachers College. Our special joy in creating this development project is that it is the product of collaboration between practicing classroom teachers in Central and West Harlem and preschool classroom and university specialists—specialists not only in curriculum design but in science, mathematics, and music. The result is a day-by-day, week-by-week, month-by-month structuring of what the teacher might do to diagnose the capabilities of a child and to reinforce them in a noncompetitive and free setting.

The C.H.I.L.D. Project is now close to completion, and we have discovered that teachers themselves hunger for this type of structuring, as long as it is not coercive and is not handed down by school administrators. All the talk about resistance to innovation has diminished as teachers become acquainted with this program, which is less theoretical than many of the early childhood programs, much more specific in structure and more generous in its provision of equipment to teachers. We expect to disseminate this highly structured program on a national basis shortly.

Another project, the Language Acquisition Project at the center has given us new encouragement. Here, we use applied linguistics, and applied psycholinguistic procedures while working with children from a tenement apartment house in the most impoverished neighborhood of Bridgeport, Connecticut. It is an effort to encourage children to play language and speech games with one another, with their high school age brothers and sisters, and with their mothers. We have trained paraprofessionals and classified them under arrangements in Connecticut as "Language Nurses." We have developed a highly structured arrangement for shaping local dialect into standard school English dialect in a way which is pleasurable, but guarantees in advance some success for the preschool child.

There is still more evidence of the importance of preprepa-ration. Among the many evaluations of Title I and Title III projects that we have completed over the last three years at the center, only six projects designed by professional educators exhibit any evidence of positive gains in students. Among these I would include the New York City Junior High School Sum-mer Program, a semitutorial program, which has shown demon-strable gains because it is highly structured and the teachers who agreed to take part followed prescribed routine of instruc-tion. I expect teachers who have great belief in creative potentiality to be appalled by my repeated emphasis on struc-ture. I would encourage such individuals to restrict themselves to the affluent, suburban schools.

Upward Bound has had success because it has concentrated on increasingly structured situations that are a preliminary preparation for college-level performance. The problem with the Higher Horizons Program was that it enriched the student but it did not provide him with academic skills. Higher Hori-zons, in a three-year, follow-up evaluation, was shown to yield no effects, primarily because the enrichments of visits to cul-tural institutions were not preliminary preparation for mastery. They did not provide advance mastery of skills in subject areas. They enriched in general, which was of little use in compen-sating for disadvantage.

The "during" stage is my second element. The disadvan-taged student is one who is least equipped to compensate for poor instruction. The advantaged student has built up a whole repertory of skills to counteract poor instruction. For example, our great land grant universities offer elaborate, often endowed, fraternities and sororities which are compensatory mechanisms for poor or irrelevant instruction. A student can specialize in his fraternity affiliations. This, I submit, is an example of a compensatory adjustment to the learning situation on the part of the student. It is an illustration of the private cultivation of special skills.

However, the disadvantaged student lacks the access to his peers that would allow him to compensate for dull or irrelevant instruction in the same way the socially advantaged student does. Also, the disadvantaged student cannot compensate by cultivating the same range and quality of private skills. There are, of course, exceptions to both statements. Sometimes the peer learning of the disadvantaged student exceeds in quality anything that the advantaged student ever dreamed possible in range of contact, in depth of personal exploration and discovery, and in the build-up of loyalties.

But that is a disadvantage because it contains no educational dividend and, therefore, extensive peer learning in the neighborhood setting may be a further disadvantage to the pupil since it is not the kind of learning that is as acceptable even as the fraternity type of learning happens to be in the land grant university. To put it another way, it is acceptable to be a pompom-twisting cheerleader in a white ghetto suburb, but it is socially unacceptable to be a member of a "bopping" gang in the ghetto streets.

It is also the case that the disadvantaged student develops special private skills—sometimes very impressive ones—but, again, socially unacceptable in the school context. The type of musical instrument learned is one that the high school music department considers taboo. For example, one local school system is now admitting electronic instruments to its pool of acceptable musical devices for the first time. More important is the fact that some of the skills acquired by the disadvantaged student cannot be developed in quite the same way because of limited resources. It is harder to "turn off" in school and then find the money and the leisure arrangements that would enable one to cultivate himself as a figure skater or even a karate expert. Karate lessons cost a great deal of money.

We have found some solutions to this "during" problem. Consider one piece of evidence: three years of sustained research on the More Effective Schools program, in spite of all the political conflicts that have surrounded these evaluations, suggest that the More Effective Schools, thus far, are not more effective primarily because they do not modify the minute-by-minute behavior of teachers in classrooms. Class size has been reduced, released time that is of vital importance to teachers has been increased, parent aides are available, better audio-visual equipment is at hand—all of those factors are of tremendous importance. But in the midst of it is a teacher who has not been provided with the means to modify the teaching method used when she had thirty-six pupils in the classroom, no released time, no equipment, and so forth. In this sense, poor instruction continues, and the student remains at a disadvantage because his compensatory alternatives are restricted in the manner mentioned earlier.

The greatest achievements in research and development since 1965 are coming into focus around this subject of what happens in enclosed classrooms in ghetto schools from 9 A.M. to 3 P.M. I am tremendously excited by the development of the Individually Prescribed Instructional (IPI) System of Research for Better Schools Incorporated, the regional laboratory in Philadelphia. IPI has spread from three experimental schools to one hundred schools ranging from the Harrisburg slums to Minnesota. The point of interest to me as an educational developer is that IPI modifies the minute-by-minute philosophy of action in the classroom. The group-competitive basis is eliminated. The child learns against his own standard and at his own rate. This is vital to the so-called disadvantaged child because we think, in the IPI arrangement, which is partly programmed instruction, that the child does not have to compensate for poorly designed or irrelevant instruction of the kind that those students who are advantaged have endured with such resilience for so many years.

There is another way in which poor instruction can be modified through research and development. We feel we have accomplished some of this, in collaboration with New York City elementary and junior high schools, in the creation of the beginnings of a social education program. What we have found in three years of experimenting is that there are ways of instigating field work and neighborhood participation in field research and city planning into even the fourth and fifth grade levels of neighborhood schools. We have found means of intriguing elementary and junior high school students with the problems faced by their local government, by their neighborhood leadership groups; we have used the participatory democracy theme to try to increase the relevance and thus, the instructional impact of early social studies. Yet, the same schools are presently devoid not only of sex education information, to which I would give comparatively low priority, but of information on applied law.

Local law—not merely civil rights and civil liberties law, but precinct level law—is missing from the social studies curriculum at the elementary and junior high school level. This subject provides the kind of information on survival which is supplied in abundance in the affluent suburban home.

We think the same kind of structuring used in the minute-by-minute program can be found in the bilingual educational approaches that are beginning to reach the cities. This is mainly the result of the work being carried on at the University of Texas and the Southwestern Regional Educational Laboratory. Language instruction can be highly structured, even at the early level, and this is especially true of bilingual instruction.

We also think that students can compensate for poor instruction through the resources that come into play by participating in citizen determination of some of the policies bearing on neighborhood schools. In other words, if you want to ask what the importance of citizen participation and community control is, one of the answers is that it is an alternative to poor instruction. It provides an increase in relevant experiences, even in school systems where the instruction is distinguished by its inadequacy—as in West Virginia, where community control has flourished for many decades.

We have begun to be interested at the center in what our collaborator in this project, Milton Galamison, called "fun and games." What we are interested in is the fact that the skills children in the ghettos develop privately, the games they play and learn to play so well, can be redesigned and modified into educationally relevant experiences. We are following here a tradition that built up in the kibbutz where children's games were catalogued and put down in words that could be used in terms of instructional interest across the State of Israel. These games in the forms used in Israel are not transferable to the American urban scene, but we are looking for parallels and equivalents. We are asking children to try out foreign games and make their own variations and modifications, which they are well-equipped to do. One result of this may be to make the after-school programs now available in the urban educational system more stimulating.

Finally, just a few more words about the "after" phase. By the "after" phase I mean simply that our notion of the advantaged student is one who knows what to do when he has the credentials in hand. Nearly anyone can graduate from Princeton, but it takes a Princeton man to know what to do with the diploma. Most contemporary professions have meetings to discuss ways of exploiting their professional credentials. How do you utilize the fact that you have been certified? Education, contrary to the romantic yearnings in this regard of Paul Goodman, is a certifying process. How do you take advantage of having been certified?

The disadvantaged pupil is one who does not know or who is not well positioned enough to exploit the credentials. Never mind his academic training. He does not have the fraternity contacts or the equivalent in working-class circles—the uncle in the union. The people he does know will protect him against being exploited, but they do not know how to exploit somebody else, except in the sense of neighborhood hustling.

There are efforts being made to change this. In Westchester County's OEO program, there has grown up a private corporation called "College Careers." This corporation has been in operation for three years and to date it has a 90 percent success rate. What "College Careers" says to the clients, nearly all of whom have records as criminal delinquents or high school dropouts or both, is the following: "If you enter this program, you go to college and you graduate and we fit a college to you." The program consists of making that arrangement and then staying with it and making all the other arrangements required to help a person for four years until he is certified as a college graduate. This is a social casework arrangement and it is a great asset. It is precisely what our uncles and aunts, mothers, fathers, and grandfathers did for us.

The College Careers Program is not a preparatory remedial or Upward Bound or SEEK style program. It is a program which is at base social work in that the pupil is located, his disposition to go to college considered, and on the basis of motivation alone, the student is placed in the college. Every effort is made on his behalf to give him the support necessary to make it through college and to be his advocate in facing the administration, the faculty, and parents. It is a different strategy, but one that conveys my emphasis on arrangements. For example, if a student "gets busted" for smoking marijuana two semesters after his placement in a college, College Careers does not say "You have lost; you've just been disqualified." It says, "Well, now you've been busted. Let's see, what legal arrangements are necessary." Whatever these are, they are provided and the student is subsequently readmitted to college. The 90 percent success is not success on four-year programs. (Some programs such as the one at Antioch College for the advantaged student, take seven years to complete.)

Another illustration revolves around a training project for young adults, which, it is hoped, will equip them for becoming neighborhood planners and community organizers under the Restoration Corporation in Bedford-Stuyvesant. When the Restoration Corporation was just beginning, two of its officers conveyed the impression to the trainees that they would be placed in jobs upon completion of the training process. That became the main consideration of the course, which was six months in length. Four and one-half months into the training process it became evident that there might be no jobs to be distributed. Demoralization, frustration and anger became extreme. It occurred to me that as an advantaged upper middle-class expert in credential exploitation, I would never have entered such a project without advance evidence of the job placement. Nor would I have entered the training projects unless I had been guaranteed "credits." In the case of educating the disadvantaged, these little details which the rest of us insist upon, are often forgotten. For education of the disadvantaged to succeed, whether it is a work-study program or a neighborhood youth-corps-school collaboration, there must be aftermath arrangements which enable the youth to exploit new opportunities. These do not have to be delivered paternalistically. I am not talking about patronage arrangements. I am not talking about the provision of *phony* rewards such as embossed, gold starred graduation certificates. I am talking about the provision of specific opportunities which can be pursued by the individual.

I have tried to suggest that educators believe something about the successful teaching of the disadvantaged has been learned. I have not gone into the depressing evidence that would suggest that the research and development community have not yet learned nearly enough. But, some approaches have been found which we think would unlock the mystery of "How to instruct effectively." In unlocking this mystery, we could make a major contribution to the solution of a national problem.

5

Moderating Conflicts through
School Public Relations

DOYLE BORTNER

Schools cannot avoid public relations. The people develop and express opinions concerning their schools whether or not school officials take action to interpret them to the public. Thus, public relations is not an option. The only option is whether school public relations will be planned or accidental, organized or slipshod.

Few educators would argue with the validity of this statement. Yet, some continue to neglect the needs for organizing planned public relations programs. Few would be undisturbed by evidence of public misunderstanding and dissatisfaction. Yet, some continue to permit communication concerning the schools to escape from their leadership and control. Few would debate the need for public support for public education. Yet, some appear to expect support without positive efforts to win it.

Whatever the reasons for neglect of planned and organized programs of school public relations, the fundamental error lies in failure to understand that no institution in a free society can prosper without public understanding and support. The business community has long understood this, as witnessed by their advertising, research and services, reports to stockholders, and other activities that come under the rubric of highly organized public relations. If public relations are important to business, how much more important is it to schools that are of immediate concern to almost every home through the children or the tax bill.

Nevertheless, most schools were caught short (that is without public understanding and support) during the great depression of the 1930s with the result that their budgets, staffs, facilities, and programs were often cut without mercy and without popular protest. Many were again caught short during the post–World War II period when the people were slow to react to the most critical needs for staff recruitment and building programs. Many were once again caught short by the launching of Sputnik by the Russians when public opinion was easily rallied against the schools by those looking for easy answers to the reasons why we failed to beat the Russians. And today some schools continue to be caught short by the conflicts of a very rapidly changing society, particularly of urban society, and by the tendencies of many people—often with good reason but just as often with oversimplified answers to exceedingly complex problems—to blame the schools for the conflicts or as being responsible for their solution. Happily, there is reason for cautious optimism, for it is clear that increasing numbers of schools and school districts understand the need for school public relations programs and have developed or are in the process of developing organized programs to meet these needs.

Despite the needs for and potential contributions of school public relations in moderating conflicts in education, it is important to emphasize, before proceeding further, that no claim can or should be made for school public relations programs as a panacea for educational problems. Production necessarily precedes salesmanship, and this is as true in education as it is in business and industry. There is no point, indeed, there is no morality, in trying to "sell" the people on a program of educational production which does not, in fact, exist. At the same time, school public relations are not synonymous with a good school program, an oversimplified view of some school personnel. Important as a strong school program is to good public relations, there remains the need to tell the people about it, to help them understand it, and, most essential, to involve them in partnership efforts to develop and support it. As Abraham Lincoln said: "With public sentiment, nothing can fail. Without it, nothing can succeed."

Exactly what is meant by the term "school public relations"? Before answering this, it might be well to consider what it does not mean, for the term does tend to imply erroneous and unfortunate concepts in the minds of some laymen and, indeed, some educators. First, it is not a high-pressure campaign, a bag of tricks designed to lubricate the gears of public consent, to sell the people on something they do not understand or want. Neither is it simply another name for publicity or advertising, for publicity alone overemphasizes one aspect of school public relations associates with press agentry, while advertising overemphasizes sales of school propositions. While these approaches have been used in the guise of school public relations the results have generally been unsatisfactory. If public relations does have such implications in the minds of many people, it is all the more necessary for school public relations to develop an identity of its own. This identity needs to accent the promotion of understanding between the schools and the public through a two-way process of interpretation. In such a context school public relations can be defined as a series of planned activities and media through which the schools seek to learn about their community, inform the community about the purposes, programs, and problems of the schools, and involve the community in planning and evaluating school policies and progress. Such a definition makes it clear that school public relations is a two-way street. It means understanding the public so that the public can be helped to understand the schools; it means listening as well as talking.

Actually there are three levels of school public relations. The lowest level, but still an improvement over the "do nothing" apathy of some schools, is that of publicity or information giving. The next level is that of interpretation, which combines publicity and information giving with efforts to explain, educate, and persuade. But the highest level is that of interaction, superimposed upon a program of information giving and interpretation. Far from being an idealistic concept, this level of operation recognizes the hard fact that public understanding and support are best assured when schools not only keep the people informed but also seek to keep them involved. It is the only level of operation that, realistically, offers a good chance of contributing to the moderation, possibly even the solution, of conflicts in urban education.

If the highest level of public relations is to be realized, the public relations program must be planned and organized with the goals of information giving, interpretation, and interaction in mind. This in turn, means that the media and techniques of public relations must be selected, not because they strike someone as imaginative, or because other schools or school systems are employing them, but because they implement basic concepts, or guidelines established in advance as being essential to the realization of program goals. Concepts are important to the success of a public relations program in much the same way that strategy is important to an army. It is doubtful that an army could achieve victory by simply using a mass of tactics without any overall strategy. Yet, school personnel too often choose public relations tactics without attention to guiding concepts, a practice not likely to contribute much of long-range significance in solving educational conflicts. What, then, are some of the major concepts essential to the success of a public relations program attuned to information giving, interpretation, and interaction?

As a concept of first importance, school public relations should be based upon recognition of the fact that public schools belong to the public. This concept, widely accepted in theory, is still not clearly understood by many professional educators; a situation which in itself has motivated or heightened many of the conflicts in education, especially in urban centers. Yet, the concept is simple enough. It means that in a free society the people retain control of public policy, including public educational policy. It means that the people are "stockholders" owning the schools, not spectators looking on from the outside. In a larger sense it means that professional educators have a unique responsibility for strengthening democracy by practicing democracy. It means, further, that there should be a clear understanding between professional educators and the public concerning their respective roles in policy making and policy implementation, an understanding essential for good education and the avoidance of conflict.

As a second concept, school public relations should facilitate a two-way or circular flow of information between schools and community. As Oliver Wendell Holmes said: "To be able to listen to others in a sympathetic and understanding way is perhaps the most effective mechanism in the world for getting along with people and tying up their friendship for good."

Third, participation in decision making is the surest route to understanding and support. People who participate may temporarily be more difficult to work with but, in the end, will usually work harder for better school programs. Of course, where participation is encouraged, its products must be utilized as fully as possible; otherwise indifference or outright antagonism may quickly emerge.

Fourth, public relations must be directed at all the publics of the school community. There are a number of publics representing various vocational, income, educational, cultural, racial, religious groups, parents and nonparents. Successful public relations must involve all of them, not simply selected interest groups.

Fifth, a public relations program must be continuous. A continuing program is a prerequisite to continuing interest, understanding, and support. There may appropriately be changes of pace but these changes should be parts of a total plan, not campaigns to arouse public concern except in times of crisis in the schools.

Sixth, public relations must be honest in purpose and implementation. This is a matter of practicality as well as morality. While the public is sometimes generous in forgiving mistakes, even an occasional stupidity, it never forgives dishonesty. Some educators, in an understandable anxiety to win support, tend to give the public a distorted impression of school achievements. No school or school system is without its shortcomings; and if honest enough to admit them the school will appear more human and probably win greater support.

Seventh, informational materials should be adjusted to the level of the public for whom they are intended. Some messages are directed to the total community, while others are directed only to certain of the publics; and their interests, concerns, and educational levels should be considered in developing the language and medium of communication.

And eighth, personal contact should have priority over all the more impersonal media and techniques in building school public relations. Without underestimating the need for and potential of publications, newspaper publicity, audio-visual devices, and formal kinds of associations, there is little question but that attitudes and opinions are influenced most strongly by direct person-to-person contacts. This, in turn, stresses the need to make every member of the school staff a member of the public relations team through in-service education in his responsibilities and opportunities to promote understanding and respect.

So defined and so conceived, school public relations, when implemented through a functional organizational structure for the system at large and its individual school components, should contribute substantially to the fulfillment of specific requirements, to the satisfaction of particular needs, without which the stage is set for conflict in education. What are these requirements or needs that can be met through a public relations program and, conversely, are likely to remain unmet or to be met haphazardly in the absence of a planned program?

Most important is the need to develop awareness of the significance of education to the successful functioning of democratic society. While this need may seem so obvious as to be hackneyed, the fact is that educators, by failing to persuade the public of the need for quality education for all the children of all the people, have in the recent past been pushed to the wall by critics who in the name of "excellence" have called for an educational system geared to the intellectually and, often, the socially and economically elite.

Perhaps a more immediate need to be met through a public relations program is the discharge of the Board of Education's legal and moral responsibility to render an account of its stewardship; that is, to tell how it is educating the children and spending the money entrusted to its care. It would also fulfill the need to promote understanding of an increasingly complex educational program. When one considers that the process of change in education is in its most crucial period in history, that the school is teaching children of this generation to take their places in a future generation, it is clear that citizens who recall their educational programs of a previous generation will often need help in understanding the modern school.

Clearly, a basic need to be fulfilled through a public relations program is the provision of a system that will generate participation by all segments of the public or by their representatives in the development of educational policy. Democracy demands faith in the ability of an informed people to make intelligent decisions. Even though it sometimes results in sluggish operation, there is no safe alternative, for educational policy is public policy of the greatest importance. It determines, in large measure, what kind of nation, indeed, what kind of cities we will fashion, and what kind of adults our children will become.

There are, of course, numerous other important requirements or needs to be met by programs of school public relations. In overly abbreviated fashion they can be listed as follow: (1) to foster confidence in the schools and appreciation of their accomplishments; (2) to win adequate financial support—a materialistic but realistic need if schools are to compete successfully for the tax dollar; (3) to compete for the public's attention—no simple task amid the many demands and attractions of modern life; (4) to cope with criticism, not by smothering it but by welcoming it as an opportunity to build constructive relations through analysis of objective, factual information; (5) to deal with rumor and propaganda, both of which are apt to flourish in a vacuum of accurate information; (6) to meet the challenges of pressure groups that would use schools to reach their own selfish ends, groups that usually thrive in an atmosphere of public indifference but which can be restricted to legitimate roles as minority interest groups if schools have the support of a concerned and understanding public; (7) to create an atmosphere conducive to change and progress in education, for change and progress is unlikely in the face of an unreceptive or antagonistic public; (8) to establish the framework for cooperative and coordinated efforts with community organizations; (9) to foster favorable attitudes toward teachers and other school personnel—a need likely to be met not only through effective teaching and service but also by making the public aware of effective teaching and services; (10) and to develop thorough understanding of the community with which the schools are working, for schools can neither best serve or communicate with their communities unless they know them intimately.

Without discounting the needs for public relations programs in school districts of all sizes, it is clear that the needs are today generally most critical in the large urban school districts. Not only does the urban district face problems that are greater in size but it also faces problems that are unique in nature. Certainly it would be presumptuous and unduly time consuming to attempt a detailed review of these problems with an audience of this nature. A listing would very likely include the problems of the cities (sociological, economic, geographic, and political) as well as those that are more specific to the schools, for the schools feel the weight of all urban problems. The schools and their public relations plans and programs are bound to be affected by the very acceleration of urbanization; the development of segregated pockets of economic and cultural deprivation; rapid population mobility; housing decay and new patterns of communal living, and the accompanying social problems of family life, health, and crime in ghetto environments. At the same time, problems relating more specifically to school organization and operation in the largest of our urban communities have important implications for the creation of public relations difficulties and efforts to resolve them. While not universally attributable to all large urban school districts, it is fair to mention here the problems of: (1) overcentralization—making it most difficult to disseminate information and involve citizens in policy development and problem solving; (2) suspicion of school personnel due to ethnic or cultural differences or, perhaps, simply traditional distrust of authority figures; (3) ineffective educational leadership, by virtue of training, experience, or personal qualities, on the part of *some* school administrators, in dealing with new problems of urban society; (4) excessive enrollments in individual schools and subdistricts; (5) ineffective political and fiscal solutions in the face of available federal and state resources; (6) inadequate understanding of students, their families, communities, homes, problems, aspirations, and frustrations on the part of some teachers and administrators; (7) curricular programs that have tended to favor the children of professional managerial, white-collar type parents, of the more culturally advantaged; (8) and recruitment of an adequate number of teachers prepared for and dedicated to service in urban (including ghetto) schools.

Obviously there are no simple or ready-made solutions to these problems and to others that beset the urban schools. Then, too, solutions that work in some instances may not work in others, for urban communities and neighborhoods differ greatly, despite many common problems. In any event, it is not the purpose here to outline tentative solutions to the problems of our great urban communities and their school systems. Discussion of decentralization, revision of the fiscal base for school support, curriculum development, recruitment and assignment of staff, and many of the other measures that can contribute to the solution of problems and conflicts lie well beyond the scope of this presentation. Yet, whatever solution is implemented, it will be successful only to the degree that school public relations are conducive to a joint approach, a cooperative effort; for no solutions can succeed in an atmosphere of misunderstanding, discord, or animosity. Further, some of the problems and the conflicts are essentially problems of public and school relationships. On these two scores, therefore, that which has been said concerning the nature, concepts, and potential contributions of programs for school public relations has pertinence.

As I have stated above, the successful attainment of the highest level of public relations also demands a careful selection of the techniques and media to be used. These should help to promote understanding and support of urban schools serving economically and culturally depressed areas and, more important, to foster an atmosphere of good will and partnership between school and community. Actually, these means and media are basically the same as those that are useful in all kinds of communities but with appropriate adjustments and emphasis. Following are a few examples of approaches that can be used successfully.

Of all means and media, personal contacts, as indicated earlier, are of prime importance. This is especially true in depressed urban communities where immediate contacts are likely to be much more meaningful, perhaps more acceptable, than are more formal programs, or printed materials. Only through personal contacts can views be exchanged effectively, can issues be explained in such a way as will assure understanding, and can warmth, interest, and concern be effectively reflected. Only through personal contacts can the reticence of many people to attend and participate in formal programs and the inability to read or comprehend written materials be offset. Although the most productive kinds of personal contacts are often unplanned and unstructured. Those encouraged by an open-door policy in the schools and chance meetings on the street, in stores, at social affairs, and the like can also be effective. The schools need to create more structured arrangements for individual and group contacts if public relations are not to be left to accident, if opportunities for personal contacts are to be effectively provided, if partnerships of understanding and effort are to be purposefully motivated.

Perhaps one of the best examples of opportunities for establishing contacts, at least with parents, is through the conference procedure for reporting pupil progress. The advantages of the person-to-person conference should be apparent from both the diagnostic and the parent relations viewpoints. Properly managed, the conference makes it possible to give detailed, on-the-spot explanations, to correct misunderstandings, to allay suspicions, to ease ruffled feelings, and to foster aspirations for children and positive attitudes toward the school. At the same time, the usefulness of the conference as an instrument of diagnosis and parent relations emphasizes the need for adequate time and skillful handling, factors that, in turn, suggest the need for careful administrative planning, thorough in-service training for teachers, and advance orientation for parents.

Informative and meaningful procedures for reporting pupil progress, always important, are particularly important in the case of parents who may not be so well educated or self-assured as their counterparts in more privileged communities. Schools serving depressed urban areas have special responsibilities for assuring the clarity of pupil progress reports and, further, for assuring that the reports are neither threatening nor affronts to human dignity.

In addition to inviting parents to the schools for conferences on the progress of their children, parents as well as other citizens in depressed urban areas can be invited, just as are their counterparts in more favored communities, to serve as resource visitors. It should not be assumed that they have nothing worthwhile to contribute simply because they are economically and educationally below par. Many have interesting hobbies or talents, have lived in distant places, have served in the armed forces, or the like, and the learning process, positive attitudes toward the school, and self-esteem can be enhanced when they are sought out and invited to serve as resource visitors.

Other means of bringing parents and the community's citizens into the schools, thereby establishing a base for personal contacts, are through meetings and programs specifically designed to serve their needs. These might include parent education classes, functional parent association meetings, and adult education and recreation classes and projects.

Parent education classes could conceivably cover as wide a range of topics, for example, from nutrition to budgeting, as are consistent with the interest and needs of parents whose children attend the schools. Of particular significance, however, are classes concerned with child development and learning processes designed to foster higher levels of aspiration for their children, and, in so doing, more positive attitudes toward the school as their partner in achieving these aspirations. This process is best begun with parents of preschool children and continued thereafter without interruption through the secondary school where, through tradition or lethargy, there is often an interruption in parent-school contacts. This occurs at the very time that parents, particularly those in depressed urban areas, should be learning of the possibilities and accessibility of higher education for their children.

Closely related to the above approach are functional parent association meetings; functional in the sense that they are attuned to the real needs and interest of parents and their children and can draw parents into the school. Indeed, the school located in a depressed urban area may have a built-in advantage, since its parents have fewer competing attractions or commitments and less money to spend on commercial amusements. When such meetings are thoughtfully planned by parents and school personnel, supported by the attendance and participation of teachers and administrators, devoted to practical working sessions, they can engage the interest of parents, become a forum for personal contacts, and help school personnel to gain clearer insights into the community, its resources as well as its trouble spots. Clearly, such meetings are in sharp contrast with the "ladies-aid society," fund-raising nature of too many parent association meetings.

The use of adult education and recreation programs and projects, while beneficial in almost any community, are almost indispensable in economically deprived urban areas. Of course, decisions on kinds of opportunities to be provided should be based on a survey of community needs and interests and of the possibilities for cooperative and coordinated efforts with other community agencies. Besides contributing to the solution of community problems, the upgrading of individual skills, and the productive use of leisure, these programs and projects can promote good school public relations by attracting citizens into the school, motivating personal contacts between participants and school staff members who are involved, and building respect for education as a functional response to problems, needs, and interests.

Despite the potential values of parent conferences, parent education classes, parent association meetings, invitations to serve as resource visitors, and adult education and recreation programs, it would be naive to assume that parents and citizens of the depressed urban community will respond with enthusiasm and unanimity. Their participation will likely depend upon their involvement in planning and evaluating stages. Without such participation, reaction may often be one of disinterest, doubt, cynicism, or apprehensiveness. In a larger sense, the personal involvement of participation in decision-making processes is the most fruitful means available to urban schools for the creation of citizen understanding and support. As previously emphasized, this participation, to be significant, must relate to the development of basic educational policies, not simply to the planning of matters of marginal importance. Certainly, the need for organized citizen participation in the affairs of schools serving depressed urban areas is especially critical because of past neglect, the reticence of some, and the present-day militancy on the part of many others. Representative advisory committees of parents within individual schools and of citizens within subdistricts of the school system, as well as committees for the school system as a whole, all organized according to specific bylaw provisions, must be authorized to work with school authorities in achieving concrete and meaningful goals. That such committees can make significant contributions to both good education and good school public relations is underscored by the experiences of hundreds of committees (largely, but not entirely, in suburban and other more modestly sized school systems) since World War II. Without such committees, there is less likelihood that the educational interests and concerns of low-income groups will be either heard or protected. In order to assure that the committees are truly representative of the community, the need for a community survey is once again apparent, for only the survey can give accurate information on population composition, organizational structure, and leadership. Only by scientifically and democratically organizing the committees is it possible to assure that committee control, by default, will not be left to a possibly militant minority.

This very brief review of a few of the means and media available for promoting understanding and support of urban schools and (by implication) for moderating conflicts in education should not be viewed as suggesting that many additional approaches, including many traditionally associated with public relations, are of little importance. Indeed, one means, that of reversing the process of bringing parents and citizens into the schools by sending staff members into the community for purposes ranging from home visitations to participation in community organizational life has not been considered, although such activity would have to be an important part of a total school public relations program. Neither has attention been given to the many possibilities of printed media of communication such as newspaper publicity, including publicity in the foreign language newspapers—often widely read in certain urban areas, regular and special school publications, and student publications. Nor has attention been given to many of the nonprinted media of communication including films, filmstrips, recordings, exhibits, demonstrations, speakers bureaus, special campaigns, and, indeed, the whole range of the student activities program that can often play a significant role in interpreting the schools. Finally, no attention has been given to the important and specific roles of particular personnel, that is, members of the board of education, the superintendent, the principal, the director of public relations, the teacher, or the member of any one of the various professional and nonprofessional units of the school staff in the promotion of school public relations. Only a thorough study of school public relations could possibly analyze its potentialities for moderating educational conflicts. Nevertheless, I hope that this presentation has testified to the fact that these potentialities do exist.

6

Improving School-
Community Relations

ELLIOTT SHAPIRO

The history of school and community relationships has probably been a long one. I use the word *probably* because for much of this history, the relationship has been so tenuous that it often seemed to be nonexistent. If you think back to the days when you were in elementary school and think about the community-school relationships that existed then, you would probably join me in asking, "What do you mean by community-school relationships? Did your mother dare to come to school? How many meetings did your mother or your father attend in the schools? Did your mother or father go to school only when somebody sent for them? If you were a good child, your mother and father were never called to the school." If you think of community-school relationships, you will remember your graduation, when there was perhaps a gala pageant at which you portrayed the spirit of clean teeth. At this point, mother and father came in very proudly and probably did not indicate to anyone that you were a hypocrite because you did not want to brush your teeth in the morning or at night. Thus, in a sense, when one talks about school-community relationships, one talks about something that has, in a sense, been quiescent until very recently.

Consider what the range of activities of parents' associations in New York City and in other cities around the country has been. These were activities that evoked the stock response "Oh, she goes to PTA meetings." One recognized that the mother was a diligent parent and that she wanted something more stimulating to do than playing Mah Jong. This is not to gainsay, of course, the importance of parent-teacher associations or the United Parent Associations here in New York City. They have been and continue to be very important.

Their importance lies primarily in the fact that they can act as a political bloc. PTAs throughout the country have sometimes presented themselves to political leaders as representatives of a significant proportion of the population (indeed a larger proportion than they can actually claim). And because these men are easily frightened, nobody examines the figures carefully and inflated figures are taken at face value. As a result, the parents' associations have been able to make important contributions to education, generally in the direction of additional services, such as, protesting budget cuts, demanding and getting smaller classes, requesting additional supplies, and making educational philosophy more pragmatically democratic.

On the whole, parent involvement has been a kind of sporting activity in which the parents' associations have been vigorous in representing a large number of people by sending petitions, evaluations or studies to the Board of Education, the Mayor, and so on. They have accomplished something and they certainly protected school systems against excessive budgetary cuts. The personal involvement, the spirited intervention in behalf of education, however, was more noticeable in its absence than in its presence.

In a sense, then, the PTAs were middle-income lobbyists in behalf of an inactive establishment. The school systems indicated their strength through their reliance on their proponents. They had an advantage in developing this style in that for a long time the schools were geared to children who were middle class or middle income, or to those who had middle-class and middle-income aspirations. These aspirations were buttressed by the expectation that their children could achieve success through education. On the whole, the children who remained in school did achieve this.

Let me stress, however, that we have taken it for granted that all children who attended school went through to high school. It is an ignored fact that up to recently, not every child went to school beyond the elementary grades.

I happened to be a teacher in the 1930s at the Psychiatric Division at Bellvue Hospital. If children who came to Bellvue were in trouble, I did not realize how much trouble they were in until I looked at the record cards and saw that by the time they reached grade 6B, the boys had been left back an average of six times. That meant that by the time they were in the second half of the sixth year, they had been retarded three years. These youngsters dropped out before high school. I myself went to high school in 1924 in Flatbush, a middle-income neighborhood in Brooklyn. Not all of my elementary school classmates, however, went to high school with me. Moreover, many of my former classmates, those who had graduated from elementary school with me, dropped out during their high school course.

What I am suggesting is that we had an extremely long period in America (where everything is supposed to be so equal in regard to opportunity) when youngsters who had difficulty, whether that difficulty was represented by poverty, discrimination, disabilities or retardations—or, as sometimes happens, caused by their creativity—dropped out of school in large numbers. Only 6 percent of the young people in America at the turn of the century went to high school. Ninety-four percent supposedly were, in present parlance, dropouts.

But the dropout situation was different then. For many, it was perhaps better not to go to school because there were important career opportunities in various trades, crafts, banking houses, and utilities. Interestingly enough, opportunities were not available for Jewish youngsters at that time. Jews were not being hired by insurance companies and banks. In a sense, the Jewish parent had an additional vested interest for keeping the child in school. There were fewer opportunities not based on education.

Thus, we had a number of factors that entered into a situation that led to the development of passive relationships between school and community. Among them was the fact that alternatives were available for the youngsters who were not achieving and not remaining in school. The schools seemed to know what they were doing because they were able to prove by their student body (that is, the minority that remained in school) that the children were learning to read and write. The children in high school were doing well and some even went to college. There was no body of children one could point to and say that they were not doing well, because such children left school at the end of the sixth grade. And more were leaving in the seventh, eighth, ninth, and tenth grades than were remaining in school. I am suggesting, quite arbitrarily, that the opportunity for employment without certification was an important underlying factor which prompted quiescence in school community relationships. One said he was leaving school to get a job, not dropping out. The child was not considered a dropout. The children who were achieving remained in school, so the schools seemed to be efficient. The children who were leaving for jobs were considered to be imbued with the ethic of Horatio Alger.

These schools were not any more efficient than our schools

are today. But there has been a substantial change of philosophy over the years. Many factors are involved in regard to the change in philosophy, including the disappearance of "craftsmanlike trades." Children are now being kept in school not only through elementary, junior high school and high school but through junior colleges, and four year colleges. The schools have been confronted with a challenge to which the educators had been blind. They had accepted the status quo complacently until informed by outside forces of the changing situation.

It is a serious matter that this information came, not from the educators themselves, but from the community. It was the communities who first said, "Our children are not achieving." The poorer and more discriminated against the children were, the less they were achieving (although there were exceptions). Yet the schools did nothing, except to indicate that perhaps the children were not achieving because they were culturally deprived, culturally disadvantaged, plain poor, or the parents were apathetic. It is one of the tragedies of the not too recent past that the school community did not make a consistent effort to find out what was involved in the lack of achievement.

Indeed, they moved in another direction, that other direction can be symbolized by the fact that the school people around the country defended the "Group Intelligence Test." When the people of the communities said, "You know your group intelligence tests are only reading tests and if a child cannot read, he is not going to score well. Then, when you give a reading achievement test and he does not score well, it is unfair to say he is not doing well on the reading achievement test because he scored poorly on the I.Q. test, simply another reading test."

Some community people and some people within the school system argued that since you were testing for the same thing in both tests, namely achievement rather than ability, it was improper to accept that test as an indication of ability. But the school system had a vested interest. An efficiency ratio was even developed. If the children in a school were testing at a certain academic level and if the average I.Q. of a school were at a certain intelligence level—the achievement level was compared to the I.Q. level—the school got a rating. Virtually every school had a rating between .93 and 1.03, with 1.0 meaning an exactly equal rating between achievement and the I.Q. scores. One will realize that those that scored 1.01, 1.02 or 1.03 had youngsters who were reading somewhat higher than expectancy. But I stress that the scores hovered between .93 and 1.03 within a .10 point range, with almost all of them at about 1.00. This indicated, of course, that we were testing the same thing, though we called one thing "intelligence" and the other "reading achievement."

The fact is that educators disgraced themselves in New York City and all around the country by continuing to demand group intelligence tests because it served vested interests to demonstrate that the schools were efficient. All educators share in this disgrace. The group intelligence test has disappeared in New York City, which is now, in a sense, less benighted than most of the country, where it is still being given. It is to the glory of the New York City educational system that it finally did drop this type of test. New York, however, did not give it up willingly. The professional staff did not hesitate to label as dull, whole groups of youngsters with I.Q.'s of 83, 84, 85 or 88. This justified a 4.3 reading average in the sixth grade as not being so bad. It meant teachers were doing as well as could be expected, considering the fact that the youngsters supposedly had I.Q.'s of 83, 84 and 85.

It is to the credit of people within the communities, of some people within the school systems, and of the poor of this generation that they were not going to accept what other generations had accepted. This generation of the poor and discriminated against said, "Abolish the I.Q. tests! Prove that you know what you are doing."

We have not been able to prove it. Nor have we been able

to prove that, given certain disadvantages of discrimination and poverty and bad housing and all other kinds of distress, that we who worked or are working with children from such environments know how to reach them so they can learn at the average achievement rate in this country. Because of this, there has been a strong conviction in the poor neighborhoods that the poor also should be involved because perhaps they know things educators do not know.

It seems quite clear that educators do not know everything. We no longer can demonstrate that with much success. Again, I want to make it clear, we are not less successful than our predecessors were in 1910 or 1920. We are probably more successful. On the other hand, our predecessors did not have to prove their successes. For one thing, the youngsters were no longer in school because they had other opportunities. Now the youngsters are in school. There were no intelligence tests in those days. Now we are equal to our predecessors. We also no longer have group intelligence tests. But we do have one different factor and that is that youngsters who are not achieving are remaining in school until the age of eighteen.

The question comes up as to why teachers—not to mention principals, superintendents and other people in the rarified atmosphere—who are now working in the schools and who have been working ten years or longer, did not act. Certainly it would have been in their vested interests to have moved in the direction of improving education. If we had moved very early for real quality improvement in educational services when this need began to be apparent in the decade from 1945-1955, we would not now have a situation that is so difficult.

Why didn't we move? We did not move primarily because we were working in a school system that supposedly was carrying on the traditions of a democratic society but which was, in reality, autocratic. It is an interesting contradiction that we could not voice meaningful opinions without being called disloyal, unwilling to accept criticism, guilty of poor judgment, or a troublemaker. We could not freely express opinions within the school system. Since we could not express ourselves, it almost seemed useless to have opinions or even ideas. In an occupational sense, we were made idiots. Men who wanted to become assistant principals would work at the acceptable levels of industrious complacency in the classroom. They would be very cooperative and do some extra work for the assistant principal. They would agree with the principal who would agree with the assistant superintendent, who would agree with the deputy superintendent, who would agree with the superintendent of schools.

Things did change, however, and this is to the credit of the people who worked so hard in those early years from about 1916 on. These people worked hard to extend democratic procedures within a structure that promoted hypocrisy. In secret meetings through the 1930s and 1940s and 1950s they organized a union. Even in its first contract this union developed grievance machinery that could have been used as the transmission belt for developing regulations, rules or even the constitution of a given school. So far, however, all the machinery is being used in the piddling sort of way that delays the development of humanistic education. But teachers had begun to get off their knees, led by the men in the junior high schools, who had the hardest jobs and were not earning enough money to support their families. Interestingly enough, at the same time, the poor and the most discriminated against—namely, the black populations of the city—had begun to get off their knees, too.

A unique opportunity was offered to us; the opportunity of making a change that could have been great and profound because both oppressed groups—both the poor and the teachers —could have formed an alliance. Of course, the black people in the community did not view the teachers as oppressed because, in the eyes of the poor, teachers had good jobs. Teachers came to school in cars. They came with fur coats. Of course, they carried shopping bags, but they wore fur coats. Their jobs were steady and their husbands were working too. At 3 P.M. they left these crowded neighborhoods and went off to middle-income neighborhoods which looked like wealthy neighborhoods to the poor. If we had explained that teachers were oppressed too, the poor might well have thrown rocks at us. But we were oppressed, relative to our calling, which is actually the transmission of the thoughts and ideas of humanity. We were oppressed because we could not be free people within the school.

But, through the union we became free. About the same time the poor were saying that they were not going to accept this low level of education any longer. Since the needs of the poor and the needs of the teachers were not only similar but also overlapping, it would not have been unexpected had we joined together in a cause, a crusade, which would have added greatly to the quality of education. We were about to do this, when, instead of clasping our hands in salutations, we hit each other. We came together and our fists clenched instead of joining.

Teacher unions, quite justifiably, had as their first goal the improvement of salaries because teacher salaries in the 1940s and 1950s were so shameful that people no longer were going into teaching. We had great shortages of teachers. We picked anybody who was "warm" and who could walk into the school and said: "He is a teacher." This was primarily because the salaries were so low that equivalent salaries could be found for jobs that did not require attending college for four years and perhaps an extra year to fulfill licensing procedures. Teacher unions had to make teaching more attractive by increasing salaries. This looked terrible to the poor. How do you explain to the poor that salaries were so low when you receive $100 a week as a beginning teacher? One cannot say this salary is low to people on welfare who can't make ends meet. Teachers were living in an apartment with a bath, and the poor were sharing a bath with four other families on the same floor.

In New York City, just as the UFT was beginning to move in the direction of expanding the services and developing an educational system, it chose a slogan that was, on the whole, insensitive, narrow, and perhaps insulting. The slogan was "Services for the Disruptive Child." Groups argued against that slogan, saying that the disruptive child meant the black child and Puerto Rican child and that it was a discriminatory and racist slogan. The very same groups are now saying, "We need services for disruptive children." At that time, however, it was seized upon within the black community, more so than in the Puerto Rican community, as a slogan that indicated bad will on the part of teachers. There finally was an explosion and the community and teachers drifted apart.

Two factors were responsible. One was that most teachers and school system never really manifested an interest in solving the problem of the disruptive child. When some teachers finally began to show an interest in the disruptive child, they did it in such an insensitive way that nobody could believe their essential good will. Another factor was that there was a vested interest among black teachers within the school system for promoting this explosion. They recognized that the licensing arrangement for promotions was a slow and tortuous process and that long lists were already in existence. As a result, black teachers, who were among the younger teachers in the system, would have to wait for a generation before they could become principals, half a generation before they could become assistant principals. The black teachers, having really the same vested interests as young teachers generally, had to find some way to contend with the professional promotion system. I think the black teachers in the Afro-American Teachers' Association seized upon this vested interest. I do not criticize them in this instance, but just as I criticize the teachers and the union, so will I criticize the Afro-American Teachers Association for failing to see that there was an opportunity for working together to make the changes in the promotional process that would not have split teachers apart. Thus, the changes came in only with difficulty, disaster and tragedy. We were all responsible for this tragic split.

It is impossible to talk about developing community relationships unless we recognize how we were involved through our errors of commission, errors of omission, our quiescence, and narrowness. The entire school system was involved in not promoting the interests of the children. We felt it was easier not to rock the boat. It was certainly safer. We had a vested interest to keep those intelligence tests to prove that the children were dull. When we came out for change, we came out with an insulting slogan. On the other hand, there were those of us who wanted to change because they wished to promote the vested interests that they were concealing from the larger community. Still others within the community wanted change in order to get power within the community.

We are all at fault. It is not worth our while for me to point out that we are all at fault unless I have an underlying premise. My premise is that educators are essentially people of good will. Because we are essentially people of good will, we can discover our faults and put them out in the open. Then, because we have our personal conscience, our social conscience, our religious conscience, and a consciousness of self—whatever all those consciences and consciousnesses mean in the total gestalt—we will find some way of opening up to those who disagree with us within the schools and, simultaneously, of opening up to those who agree and disagree with us in the community. If we can declare our deficiencies by saying, "Yes, these are our mistakes, but let's move from here," my guess is that we can then finally develop the community relationships we should have in order to make the school system a humanistic society.

We have been loyal to a system almost without knowing it. We have not said to parents: "No, we can not handle your child because we do not have the specialized services that are necessary." We can not find that warm, understanding, and firm teacher in a small class. It is impossible to find a small class today.

Let's look at this another way. A parent would come in and say: "You know my little Johnny really reads at home. I can't understand why the first-grade teacher says he can't read. I tell you he can read. He knows the letters of the alphabet. If you would give me a book to take home, I'll work with him on his reading."

The principal would say: "I would rather he did not have a book at home because he will learn by memorizing (never saying "rote" because he doesn't think the mother would understand the word). We will all become confused and we will not know if he can read." The mother looks at this principal, and although she does not know the meaning of supplementary reader, she knows that there are books of equal quality and equal achievement levels. She has the feeling that if he does memorize the book, there will also be an entirely different book and we can find out very quickly whether he is reading from memory or whether he has learned the words in the original, basic reader. She looks at the principal and thinks, "If I know this, why doesn't he?" Because she is polite, educators say she is apathetic. She knows it is hopeless to continue the discussion. She does not say a word and she leaves. When she leaves, she does not come back to parent meetings or to cake sales. She does not come back and the teachers say the parents do not care. If she does come back, she does so because she knows she ought to show her face because it will go to the credit of the child. Thus, she comes and she does not say a word and the teachers say, "See! They are not even verbal. They can't talk!" But she has taken her sounding. She has been lied to, as it were, and she knows it.

These events spread in the community very rapidly and it is an act of intelligence not to come back and be lied to again. What is the point of coming to parent meetings if nothing is going to be said that is essentially truthful and meaningful? What is the sense of discussing, once you get to a meeting? Thus, in a way, it was intelligent of the poor not to participate in the PTA. It was intelligent because there was an underlying premise that we would not tell the truth and they were right. We would not say that we had book shortages. We did not have social studies books for everybody. We had no science books, or that our math books were outdated.

It was in the 1950s that we could not tell this to parents. When one or two people did talk truthfully about this, they heard reverberations from the Board of Education. Although the mother did not know why, she knew we did not tell the truth and she left the school and never came back. The parent meetings were always small unless some school or some group of teachers went crazy because things were very bad in the school and began to tell the truth.

Gradually, after a year or two years, in one school, the parents began to realize they were being told the truth. The teachers began to go out on a limb and meetings began to be very big, sometimes embarrassingly big, even exceeding what the auditorium could handle. The school now got important support. The critical factor there was, of course, that the truth finally was being told.

I submit that *we cannot develop community-school relationships that are at all meaningful unless the truth is told.* We should tell the people in New York City that north of 125th Street, a few years ago, there were only six school psychologists and only six social workers. There are lots of truths to be told and all the truths are sad truths. Truths that indicate our liabilities rather than our assets.

We should not develop, as it were, apologetics for this, but, instead, state the facts. It is not the children who are at fault.

It is not even entirely the preparation of teachers that is at fault. It is not the poor mother who is at fault. The people who should be blamed are those who control the budget strings and those who are not opening those purses wide enough to provide the necessary services. Because they have the souls of bookkeepers, they are never going to open those bags until we all get together—teachers and parents—to insist that they be opened.

I want to suggest that even if the money came from high government sources (city, state and federal), we might not benefit because it would be coming the way milk comes to a tired infant nursing at his mother's breasts, or at a bottle. The milk comes while he is falling asleep. Consequently, we would remain sleepy, monotonous and deadly. We would not be able to develop teaching methods that are appropriate for lively children. If, however, we get together to move for change, in the very acts of getting together and getting the wherewithal to make the change possible, we would come alive. If we, the teachers, and the poor could get up off our knees, we would then deserve our children.

It is the responsibility of the less distressed to move first. Thus, it is the responsibility of the teaching staffs and the supervisory staffs of the school, the district, or of the city, to extend an open hand of friendship to the poor. The distrust has become open between the poor and the school personnel because in some way the school personnel seem to be in a favored professional position and they have achieved. It is necessary for us to show our good will and begin to invite discussions and opportunities for working with the poor. In the district that I head, I have been having numerous conferences with the principals in order to develop a spirit of openness toward the community that they serve, to indicate quickly our own deficiencies, and not to cover up the things we are failing to do. We indicate our needs, but do not use those needs as an excuse for not doing more. We have had similar discussions with staffs of our schools, but these were just one-shot affairs because we have had so many crises to keep us busy. We have had many discussions with groups within the neighborhood, offering our points of view, coming to agreements, indicating areas of disagreement, but indicating always an openness and readiness to continue discussion.

I must say in regard to a budgetary cut in New York City in 1969, that of the first seventy-five speakers that appeared at the Board of Estimate from the Boroughs of Manhattan and the Bronx, forty-four came from District 3. The suggestion that the Board of Education act as though the budget were not cut came from District 3—a suggestion transmitted by me to Borough President Sutton who transmitted it to Isaiah Robinson, a member of the Board of Education, who discussed it with other Board of Education members. There was some feeling within the district that our actions had something to do with the fact that the budget was not cut as drastically as had been threatened. The fact that we were able to get this number of parents out indicated that we have made some small progress. I do not want to overemphasize this because District 3 was small and good only in comparison to other districts. Although in an absolute sense, the district was quite small.

I agree that many cities do not have the money and that the states do not have the money. I recognize too that we have a federal administration that is going to be very slow in meeting urban needs. Just because the job is that hard, we must act soon. We must develop a crusade to get substantial and enduring Urban Grant Acts from the federal government that would be the late twentieth century equivalent of the nineteenth-century Rural Grant Acts that subsidized education in the rural areas, including even Cornell University in New York State.

We are now an urban country controlled by rural overseers. We have not been acting in sufficient strength. Federal aid is not going to be given as a matter of good will. There are differences of vested interests. The people of the rural communities are better represented, relatively speaking, in the Senate and in the House of Representatives than are the people of the cities. Moreover, we have not had a style of developing very strong popular appeal and it is time for us to develop it. It is not a question actually of good will in regard to this. It is not a question of discussion. The people want this aid and must act decisively in order to get it.

I had some personal experience in the 1930s when we participated in the first integrated march in Washington, D.C. when the WPA budget was cut by a billion dollars. The money was restored, interestingly enough, and the recession on top of the depression disappeared.

I am suggesting at this point that unless we indicate our needs dramatically we are not going to have our needs met. It is time for the people who are the second class citizens—teachers and the poor—to get first class citizenship by getting what we need from the federal government. It is not going to be given easily. Therefore, it is necessary to develop an energetic campaign in which we talk freely, openly, and honestly with the people in our neighborhoods.

We have a lot to do. Let us stop fighting needlessly; otherwise the children suffer and will continue to suffer. In a sense, we are part of a new revolution and, without frightening you, it is possible to develop a revolutionary spirit that will greatly enhance the evolution of democracy so that we can become a truly democratic society. In short, unless we talk truthfully about our deficiencies within the schools, and unless we talk frequently with our parents and with those on the staff who disagree with us in order to work out a democratic strategy for subsidizing quality education, we are going to be in explosive situations that will blow us apart.

I suggest that we in New York City owe it to our children that we come together. We owe it to the rest of the nation to be a prototype for this kind of democratic involvement.

7

Community Control of Schools

REVEREND C. HERBERT OLIVER

Community control is that phase of human government in which a community of persons takes an active part in the government of their own affairs. In its broadest sense, it extends to the total life of the community (political, economical, social, religious) and embraces the most basic needs of a well-ordered society. The basic questions facing any group of persons are: What are the group's most basic needs? How best may those needs be met?

Plato in his *Republic* and Aristotle in his *Politics* admirably addressed themselves to these considerations. But both of their systems provided for built in, natural inequalities among men, inequalities which not only tolerated slavery but required the existence of slavery as a necessary part of a well-ordered society. Inequality was seen by them not only as an economic necessity for the well-being of the state but as part of the very order of nature. If community control is seen in terms of the right of all people to self-government, then community control was no part of Plato's *Republic* or Aristotle's *Politics*; for the slave community was not considered to have the right of self-determination. At best, the political philosophy which Plato and Aristotle taught in practice served to support the control of the many by the powerful few for the benefit of the powerful few.

Hellenic democracy found expression in a prosperous and privileged citizen class governing itself and the masses; never was it expressed in terms of the broad masses determining their own future. The chief concern of Hellenic democracy was with the self-government of the privileged citizen class. Community control as seen today goes beyond the concept of a privileged group governing itself—it embraces the right of all people to share in the decision-making processes that affect their own future. Such a right is seen, not as a right conferred by a privileged class or by any governmental authority, but as a natural right belonging to every man as a gift from God.

The concept of the natural right of all men to self-government found expression in seventeenth-century European history, having roots in both the Renaissance and the Reformation. Both the Reformation and the Renaissance challenged contemporary authority with an appeal to ancient authority; the one replacing the authority of the contemporary church with the authority of the ancient scriptures, the other replacing the contemporary norms of aesthetic excellence with the norms of the ancient Greek and Roman classics. But when *some* authority is challenged, it is not unreasonable to expect the rise of some who challenge *all* authority. It would appear that the latter are simply following the principles of the former to the logical conclusions; but it is not really so. Most minds do not follow principles to their logical conclusions, but only to comfortable delusions. Then, they defend those delusions as justifiable realities until a new order comes along. Nevertheless, the challengers to all authority "made the seventeenth-century scene" and insisted that only that government is acceptable which has the consent of the governed. Political thinkers like Rousseau, Montesquieu, and Locke asserted the right of the governed to have a determining voice in the affairs of government. By the end of the eighteenth century, these ideas had become so strong as to challenge and break the authoritative class structures of the contemporary English and French governmental systems—both by violent revolutionary means. The violence by which this was achieved was not accidental. It grew out of the unresponsive character of the existing governments. When any government consistently refuses to respond to the legitimate demands of the people for meaningful reforms, it is only planting the seeds of violent revolution. Such was the case in czarist Russia when an entire governmental structure collapsed under the weight of external war and internal revolution.

One of the world's greatest political thinkers, Alexander Pushkin, asserted perhaps the most basic law of politics in saying that government rests on opinion. His *Boris Godunov* illustrates the maxim. One man starts a rumor implicating the Czar in the death of the Czarevitch and a government tumbles. It is true that Tolstoy expressed the same thought, but he derived it from his literary father, Pushkin.

During the eighteenth century, mass opinion in Western nations underwent a drastic change with the rise of a new concept of government; namely, government by the people, in contrast to the prevailing concept of government by kings and autocratic rulers. This brought about the rise of the Western democracies as we know them today. A basic ingredient of Western democracy is the right of the governed to have a voice in the government. Constitutions were drafted and approved by the people, setting limits to the powers of the government and setting forth the rights of the people which the government is bound to uphold.

The concept of community control is of the very essence of Western democracy. It is nothing more or less than local self-government. Perhaps some would even go so far as to equate community control with the concept of states' rights as espoused by Southern politicians like Governor Wallace. But while Southern politics historically has insisted on the concept of states' rights, it has also persisted in denying to millions of citizens their right to participate in the government. Thus, in the name of states' rights, they limit the right of participatory democracy to the privileged citizen class. And in doing so, they reveal the close resemblance of Southern democracy to ancient Greek democracy; a concept rejected in part by modern political thinkers. The natural inequalities accepted by Greek thinkers were rejected in part by the founders of American democracy, who insisted on the "self-evident" truths that "all men are created equal." I say *in part* because most of the founding fathers themselves had slaves in spite of their announced principles. They did not follow their principles to the logical conclusion of freedom for all men, but to the comfortable contradiction of freedom for most white men and slavery for most black men. What can be said of the Greeks that cannot be said of the founding fathers is that the Greeks at least were consistent.

It cannot reasonably be doubted that every man has the right and duty to make the choices that will determine his future. If he fails to do so, he must bear the responsibility for his failure. But to deny a man his God-given right is to deny the Creator.

It was in seeking to exercise this right and duty that a group of parents and residents in Ocean Hill-Brownsville set about to improve the quality of education in the public schools. But when parents became actively involved and elected a Governing Board to administer a cluster of eight schools in Ocean Hill-Brownsville, they came face to face with an undemocratic power structure in the city that was determined to frustrate the efforts of the Governing Board either by internal sabotage or external force, and thus deny to parents their God-given right to educate their children.

The black and Puerto Rican population had been long aware of the inadequacy of the school system, but acting individually they were unable to do anything significant about the situation. Parents wondered why children could begin school quite intelligent and eager to learn, and then become progressively more frustrated and less interested in school the longer they attended school. Purely advisory, powerless local boards appointed by a remote, central Board of Education were unable to do anything more than advise a heedless central agency—heedless, not necessarily because of lack of interest, but because the job was too big for one central agency of non-paid volunteers to administer effectively. How, in a democracy, an appointed agency could gain almost autocratic power over the lives of over a million school children and operate at times in utter contempt of the people it should be serving is an entire study in itself, which cannot be entered into now.

In a well-ordered society there are three basic spheres of influence: the church, the state, and the home. Each has its own inherent right to be; each right is derived not from either of the other two but from God. The church does not create the state or home; the state does not create the church or home; the home does not create the church or state. Each exists in its own right and has its own sphere of influence, its own inherent powers, and its own limitations.

It is the right and the duty of the church to provide for and carry out the orderly worship of God at regular intervals and to provide for the religious instruction of mankind. It is the right and the duty of the state to protect the citizen in the exercise of his rights and duties. It is the right and the duty of the home to protect and nurture the child throughout its formative period and to create and strengthen those human bonds which are necessary for the survival of any society.

It is the right (their exclusive right) and the duty of parents to educate their children. Neither the church nor the state has the right to take from the home the precious right to educate its young. Where these basic rights are not observed, there will be trouble. No select group, other than parents, has the right to educate children. No group of "educators," no union, or Board of Education has the inherent right to educate children. Only parents have this right. Parents may confer upon educators the privilege of educating their children, but never the right to do so. It is not the right, or duty even, of the state to educate children, but only to protect the citizen in the exercise of his rights and duties. Parents may make use of the state (or the church) as the means of educating their children, but the right to educate belongs exclusively to parents. *This is their right irrespective of station in life, or how much education they may have.* Only when these rights are established and protected by law may education proceed with normalcy. These are the rights for which we struggle and suffer in Ocean Hill-Brownsville.

On April 19, 1967 the Board of Education announced its public support of the principle of decentralization. Soon thereafter a group in Ocean Hill-Brownsville presented the board with a proposal which called for an experimental decentralization district to be administered by a locally elected Governing Board. The proposal was accepted in principle by the Board of Education. The Ford Foundation made a grant of $44,000 to the group to launch the project. Rhody McCoy was chosen as temporary unit administrator to organize the project during the summer for full operation in the fall. During the summer of 1967 a steering committee laid the groundwork in preparing the community for the election of a Governing Board on August 3, making use of the grant from the Ford Foundation. At this time, I was not involved in the project, but was serving on the local school board of District 17 and also as pastor of Westminster Bethany United Presbyterian Church, located within the bounds of the new experimental district. I was asked to serve on the new Board and after much thought, I agreed. The church, having an eye on community needs, agreed to allow me time to serve such needs in the schools.

On August 3 the election was held, and more than 1,000 persons voted, about one-fourth of the registered voters. In a district where the number of registered voters is the lowest in the state, and on an issue as least likely to excite public interest as the schools, the voter turnout was a remarkable success. Less than one-fourth of the United Federation of Teachers voting membership in 1968 closed the doors of nearly 900 schools to more than a million young people.

The make-up of the governing board was as follows: seven parent representatives, elected by popular ballot (one from each school); five community representatives, selected by the seven parent representatives; two representatives of supervisory personnel, elected by the supervisors; one college representative and the unit administrator, nonvoting and elected by the Governing Board. There were to have been seven teacher representatives, but by the time the strike of 1967 ended, most of the teachers in the district were opposed to the project, claiming that they were not properly informed of what was going on. On the first day of school the teachers were to elect a permanent representative from each school to serve on the Governing Board. But not a single school elected a representative to the Governing Board. Only after several weeks did a minority of teachers in only four schools elect a permanent representative to serve on the Governing Board.

During the spring and summer of 1967 the United Federation of Teachers was actively involved in the new project. I am informed that the original proposal was written by the UFT. But there were three incidents which seem to have turned the UFT against the project. First, there was the selection of the five community representatives by the seven, elected parent representatives. The UFT had expected to have a deciding voice in the selection of the five community representatives, but they had no voice at all in the selection. This is as it should be. It is not the prerogative of a union to choose community representatives. Second, there was the election of a unit administrator by the Governing Board. Two candidates were nominated: Rhody McCoy and Jack Bloomfield, a member of the UFT and principal of JHS 271. Seven UFT members were present and participated in the election under the supervision of Sandy Feldman, UFT field representative. By a narrow vote McCoy won the election. This was a victory for community control, as against union control of schools and community. I was elected chairman and Natalie Belkin, UFT representative, was elected vice-chairman.

Relations with the UFT were strained but not severed. The breaking point came during the UFT strike in September, 1967. At a meeting of the Governing Board attended by the UFT representative, it was proposed that the Governing Board support the strike and the union in turn would support the demonstration project. This proposal was turned down by the Governing Board on the ground that the right of our children to an education was not a negotiable item. This was the last meeting that the UFT representatives attended. The break was complete.

Soon thereafter, the UFT representatives who had served during the summer and early fall published a mimeographed sheet attacking the Governing Board without allowing Governing Board members the courtesy of receiving a copy. Some of the charges levelled against the Governing Board by some of the teachers were that the new project was a Black Power take-over, that we were trying to get rid of all white teachers, and that we were racists. It did not occur to them that possibly racism might have been the cause of a black and Puerto Rican community having 90 percent white teachers. Our efforts to persuade the teachers that our prime interest was in our children receiving a good education were a signal failure.

The problem of the Governing Board was how to make the

project succeed with a teaching staff of nearly 550 persons, the majority of whom were seriously misinformed at best, and downright hostile at worst. We knew that it would be a most difficult task, even if the Governing Board was officially recognized by the Board of Education, but that it would be well nigh impossible if the Governing Board was not recognized by either the teachers or the Board of Education. So we appealed to the Board of Education at an open public meeting to recognize officially the Governing Board, but the Board of Education refused to recognize the Governing Board. Instead, the Board of Education gave official sanction to the personnel chosen by the Governing Board without giving official sanction to the Governing Board itself. We knew that we were being structured for failure, with the UFT and the Board of Education working in concert to that end. Nevertheless we still attempted to do the impossible.

As the weeks and months passed we could see the effects of an uncooperative Board of Education and a majority of unsympathetic teachers. As a gesture of good will, we agreed to let teachers who wished to transfer out of the district do so, while at the same time we urged them to stay and work with us. Communications to this effect were sent to all teachers by Mr. McCoy. Yet we found that transfers were granted by the Superintendent of Schools, Dr. Bernard Donovan, sometimes in large numbers to the detriment of good order in the schools. Board of Education delays made replacements very difficult. At one time in November 1967, about seventeen supervisors left the district at the same time without prior notice to Mr. McCoy. Yet, somehow McCoy was able to keep up with the situation to prevent total chaos.

As discipline problems grew, UFT personnel in the district were busy writing about them and publishing articles discrediting community control in Ocean Hill-Brownsville. The December 20, 1967 issue of the UFT newspaper carried a long article on Ocean Hill-Brownsville with pictures of McCoy and two black principals selected by the Governing Board. An undercurrent theme in the article suggested that there was a black takeover in the district. The article did not mention the two white principals selected by the Governing Board. On January 15, 1968 when the Legislature convened in Albany, a copy of that particular issue was given to every member of the State Legislature. Apparently, Albert Shanker, President of UFT, was convinced that it would take legislative action to stop community control.

As early as January 1968, the Governing Board knew that it would take drastic action to save the district and our youth from uncooperative teachers. Meetings were held with the Board of Education time and again throughout the course of the school year in an effort to rectify a deteriorating situation. Appeals to the Board of Education, to the UFT, to Dr. James E. Allen, then Commissioner of Education in New York State, all proved to be equally unproductive. It became abundantly clear to the Governing Board that no help would be forthcoming from the responsible agencies. Nor did we ever entertain the notion of giving up our right to assure our children of a good education.

The Governing Board was very much aware of its responsibility to the community and to the young people in the schools, and it could not shirk that responsibility, even if other agencies did. So on May 7, 1968 the Governing Board met and, after long and agonizing deliberation, voted to transfer out of the district nineteen members of the teaching and professional staff, advising them to report to the Board of Education for reassignment and to the Governing Board if they wished to have a hearing. This was done in accord with Article II, Section 101.1 of the Bylaws of the Board of Education. The Board of Education could have done the same, but it refused to act. It was therefore our right to act in the interest of our children. We were careful not to attempt to fire a single teacher. To us it was a token action, for it might have been three hundred.

Our action was done quietly without notice being given to the press. Two days later when the news media said we had fired teachers, we still remained quiet. I had such faith in the news media that I was convinced that an enterprising reporter would certainly get the true story within a few days. But none came to inquire. News media continued to carry the story that we had "fired" teachers. Then we announced that no one had been fired, but the news media ignored us.

A horrible rumor had been spread by the news media, and I thought about Pushkin, and mass opinion, and the control of mass opinion; for whoever controls opinion controls the government. The Governing Board was almost carried under by the weight of false public opinion created by the news media. We then realized that the opponents of community control had very formidable and unscrupulous allies. The *New York Times* and WINS Radio were shockingly inaccurate, and at times unconscionably mendacious. It must be said, however, that reporters like Fred Feretti, Gil Noble, Murray Kempton, and George Todd upheld honorably the tradition of informing the public of differing sides of an issue with fairness and integrity. CBS Radio was more objective, and WLIB, WWRL, and WNEW presented a fairer picture to the public. A major turning point in public opinion came with the publication of the *Burden of Blame* by the American Civil Liberties Union, a full-page advertisement in the *Times* by the New York State Urban League, and the writings of Jay Epstein—all of which were favorable to the position taken by the Governing Board. Also of immense value was the demonstration at City Hall on October 4, 1968 and the march across Brooklyn Bridge with 20,000 voices chanting "Community control is here to stay." I will not list the vast number of organizations, agencies and persons who have made significant contributions to the cause of community control. I shall do so at another time, God willing.

Although community control has been presented to the public as a kind of lawless, irresponsible racist sport, those who have seen it in action know this is only a caricature conjured up by the news media and others and passed on to the public. While shallow minds delight in fabricating surprising and untold stories about Ocean Hill-Brownsville, more responsible writers will display a preference for fact rather than fancy, for truth rather than fiction. Community control of the schools is taken for granted all over the United States. But, when a group of black people or Puerto Rican people say "We are going to run our schools to improve the education of our children," then somehow it becomes racist, bad, something terrible.

For those who look upon my entering JHS 271 on November 26, 1968 as evidence of lawlessness on my part, please allow me to state that the Allen Settlement of November 18, 1968 did not forbid Governing Board members from entering the schools in Ocean Hill-Brownsville (and even if it had, it would have been unconstitutional). Entering a public building that is open to the general public is no crime; on the contrary, excluding some members of the general public while allowing others to enter is itself contrary to law. It should also be noted that at the same time I was arrested, a white woman was in the office at JHS 271 attempting to see me. Not only was she not arrested for criminal trespass, no one even asked her why she was in the building. And on the next day, I returned to the same school with several black and white clergymen for the whole day, and no one was arrested.

Let me say in closing that community control is nothing more than local self-government, the urgency and necessity of which is deeply felt in communities throughout the country. It is a fact of life and its day has come. It is a living reality in the breasts of those men and women who look with hope to a better future. All efforts to destroy it will only increase the chances of its success. While it is presently occupied with public education, it will by no means remain so occupied, but must and will spread to all areas of government. America will be a happier community because of it.

EDITOR'S NOTE: Because of the unique nature of the Ocean Hill-Brownsville Demonstration District and implications it poses for organizing school districts in other urban areas, the editors have included in this book a number of questions asked of Reverend Oliver and his answers. It is hoped that this will serve to give the reader additional insight into the Demonstration District and one of its leader.

Q. *Has community control improved the level of education in Ocean Hill-Brownsville?*

A. I do know that recent test scores indicate that some of the children's reading improved from one to two years and some more than that, just during one summer. The atmosphere has improved tremendously. People feel that they can go into the schools in Ocean Hill-Brownsville. Any parent can walk into a school. They are welcomed by the principals and not treated as if they have trespassed or as if they are on someone else's property. This is a great step forward. The performance of the children can not be determined fairly because we have not yet had a chance to operate. We must have a chance to operate to see if we can improve the quality of education. In spite of the opposition that we have had, I do feel that we have improved academic proficiency. We have a long way to go. But at least the proper atmosphere is there.

Q. *What do you mean by accountability?*

A. It simply means that the children should be learning in the schools and if they are not, there is something wrong somewhere and you have to find what it is. It can be found better by the local people on the local level than having to go through a huge bureaucracy before you can get back to the local scene.

Q. *If parents have the exclusive right to educate their children, and, we know that education is a social process, do you feel that white parents in white schools have the right to exclude Negro children from their schools?*

A. No, I do not think it follows that because parents have the right to educate their children, they have a right to exclude people on the basis of color. May I say that during the strike in Ocean Hill-Brownsville, we brought in white children from other parts of New York City to attend our schools. We have letters from these parents thanking us for the fact that their children could attend school during the strike.

Q. *What would you say were the main causes of the miserable failure of Herbert Johnson, the State Education Mediator, to resolve the crisis within the Ocean Hill-Brownsville schools?*

A. I would not say that he failed miserably. Mr. Johnson is a great guy. He is a gentleman and quite likeable. I say that in spite of the fact that he ordered my arrest. His position was "I am here simply to implement the settlement," nothing more, not to change one letter of it, simply to implement it. Our position was that it was impossible to implement that settlement.

When I say he was a gentleman, I mean we could go in and talk with him. He was open. He was available. When we went to see him, he would talk. He would reason. He would meet with the governing board, night and day. The next mediator operated from behind closed doors. He was unavailable. He had the sense of—I do not know whether to say sense of humor or gall. He told parents when they came to offer him their services in opening JHS 271 "If you people will behave yourselves, act nice, we'll open the school for you." These were the same parents to whom he gave only three minutes. This was his approach. You can see that we did not like his plantation psychology.

Q. *Can you account for some of Assemblyman Samuel Wright's criticism of the Governing Board and his subsequent resignation from the Board?*

A. I can not understand it. I really do not understand what he is after. The original suit against the original Governing Board brought up some matters that would not stand a day in court. In fact when it was first brought to court, it was not even prepared. The judge had to give the lawyers a few weeks to prepare the case against the Board. I would hazard a guess that he thinks that the Governing Board represents a threat to his political power. If that is so, he is reacting like a politician would react. We have not, however, accepted his resignation from the Governing Board.

Q. *What is the Governing Board's decision regarding a teacher's membership in the UFT or any other union of which your board disapproves?*

A. We do not have a policy of approving or not approving unions. We have never said that we disapprove of the UFT as such. When some of the teachers opened our schools in September 1968, a large number of them were UFT people. They were welcomed, and UFT members are still welcomed in the district. We simply want people who will work with us and try to bring about an atmosphere in the community that will help the teacher in the classroom.

Q. *Since you claimed that only a parent has the right to educate his child, what alternative does a parent in Ocean Hill-Brownsville have if he does not go along with the policy of the local board?*

A. If other parents in the community are dissatisfied with the Governing Board, they can certainly come to us and complain. If we do not listen, then we will not be a Governing Board very long and that is the way it should be. They have every right to make it known to the Governing Board if they have complaints and if they do not get satisfaction there they can take the fight as far as they can. We do have elements in the community that look upon us as Uncle Toms who have sold out everything. Of course, they are constantly writing against us. I do not think we are Toms.

We have not sold anything, but of course, we have not looked upon ourselves as a political group. We were not elected to go into politics but simply to administer schools.

Q. *The prolonged teachers' strikes in the Fall of 1968 were precipitated by the transfer of nineteen teachers out of the Ocean Hill-Brownsville School District in the late Spring of 1968. What were the charges against the teachers, and why were they exonerated by Judge Rivers?*

A. In the first place, they were transferred without charges. The Governing Board never filed charges against them. This was in accord with the bylaws of the Board of Education which permits transfers without charges. We have never presented charges. Unit administrator McCoy, who technically is not a member of the local Governing Board, did present charges. He did so after superintendent of schools Donovan threatened that if charges were not presented, then Donovan would fire him. So he brought charges. We all knew what the outcome would be, so we did not even try to prosecute them. We just left them alone. Of course, the newspapers used our silence to make it appear as though we did not have a case.

When you say they were exonerated by Judge Rivers, let me point out that he was not a judge. He was a retired judge. He was technically, in this case, just serving as a trial examiner, not as a judge. So the case never did go to court. The UFT never went to court with the case. But the use of Judge Rivers gave the impression that a court had exonerated the teachers. He was only a trial examiner. Superintendent Donovan acted unilaterally in appointing Judge Rivers and he got the ruling that he wanted.

Q. *Other than the introduction of Negro history into the schools, what other changes have been made in the curriculum?*

A. We have the bilingual program under Louis Fuentes at PS 155. We have five classes from the first grade in which the children and the teachers speak in both English and Spanish. This assures that a child coming here from a Spanish-speaking country does not have to sit in a class a year or two or three without understanding a thing. He continues to learn because both teacher and child converse in Spanish. This has, I believe, resulted in Spanish-speaking children who are more ready and capable to use Spanish.

Q. *Why did the demonstration districts come about?*

A. In Harlem, when the New York City Board of Education put up JHS 201, they found they could not integrate it as they had promised, with 20 percent white students being bussed in. The people then said, "We will control our own school." The struggle really began there. In the meantime the people in Ocean Hill-Brownsville presented a proposal to the Board of Education, shortly after the Board came out in favor of decentralization, which was approved in principle by the Board of Education. We went on from there. The proposal was never implemented by the legislature. We were just there and we were eventually recognized.

Q. *Does Ocean Hill-Brownsville hire unlicensed teachers?*

A. No. Unlicensed teachers have not been hired in Ocean Hill-Brownsville. They could not be paid. If parents want to get people who do not have a college degree, then this is their right. But I think most parents would want the best education for their children.

Q. *Are black teachers and students discriminated against in urban and suburban areas?*

A. Yes. Why is it that only 9 percent of the teachers in New York City are black? Why is it that most of the black teachers are concentrated in the black areas? You have "token" blacks hired in the outlying areas and when we send black children out there, their minds are conditioned to reject their heritage, or they never discuss it.

When the people of Great Neck, Long Island had a chance to express themselves at the polls they said, "We don't want your children coming out here." It is a fact that when it was proposed that the Board of Education would build high schools in certain areas in Brooklyn, not in areas where high schools are needed, but in white areas, white people came to the Board of Education and protested. When the Board of Education decided to send black kids out of Ocean Hill-Brownsville, down into the lower part of Brooklyn, into the white areas, whites said: "No, we don't want that." They protested and the Board of Education for one time showed spunk. They went ahead and did it anyway. They overruled Donovan. If you look at the map of the schools in Brooklyn, the high schools are scattered in white areas. In black areas, you have elementary schools and junior high schools, but when you get up to high school you have to go out of your community. Now change this around and have it so when white kids have to go to high school they have to come into a black community. You think about that and you will see that it does make a difference.

Q. *Do you have any evidence that the implementation of community control will make a difference in the educational improvement of that community as compared to the present regime?*

A. Yes. We feel that it has but we we would like to insist that we have never had a chance to breathe freely out there at all. We have got to have a chance to experiment. We must have a chance to fail. If you are going to send a rocket to the moon, you have got to have a chance to blow up a million dollars. We have never had a chance to operate the schools.

Q. *Now that you have these schools, how are you going about creating the good relationship between the parent and the teacher groups so that the children can now trust, not only their parents, but also their teachers?*

A. We were very conscious of this when we brought into the

district about 300 teachers last summer. We interviewed each one of them personally and explained to them what the situation was. We were glad to welcome them and we found out that these were people who wanted to come into this district, despite all the bad publicity. They still wanted to come into the community to help community control work. This rubbed off on the community. Word got around to the parents and the children making it easier for those teachers to work in the schools. When school opened, and during the whole time of the strike, students in JHS 271 were sitting down in an orderly fashion. Yet, practically the whole of the previous semester, the school was in chaos —kids throwing chairs out of the windows, destroying furniturn, setting fires. Why? This was before the transfer of 19 teachers. The majority of these teachers never recognized the Governing Board and we realized this was going to be a problem. How are you going to relate to people who do not relate to us? We could relate to the community, but not to the majority of the teachers. We found out that there was growing chaos in the schools and with this, UFT leaders were writing about it. We felt that those teachers were sabotaging the project from within and that we had to take action because we could not get anyone else to take action. It became so chaotic in JHS 271 that it was no longer a school.

Q. *If the Governing Board has community control, what protection does any teacher have in any classroom if any part of the community takes a dislike to that teacher?*

A. Let me cite an experience the Governing Board had with some teachers who were transferred out of the schools by principals, who had good reason to transfer them. These were one-year teachers. They appealed to the Governing Board and we were willing to hear them. We reinstated some of them over the objections of the principal. This is something quite new. I think the best protection of any teacher is good performance. Shame on those people who go into the field of education and handle the minds of children because they just want a job.

Q. *Are teachers responsible for the failures of black students?*

A. I never did blame the teachers completely for the whole system. This is the difficulty that blacks always run into when they try to get something done. If you try to get something done with the police department, then they say, "We are not responsible for these conditions, so do not bother us." In other words, "Leave it alone." If you go to the politicians they say, "We are not responsible for these conditions, so don't blame us. Leave it alone." Whatever group you go to, you run into the psychology that says, "You are blaming me and I am not going to take the whole blame." It is never that way. We never did and never will imply that teachers are totally responsible for the whole system. Of course they are not. But they are partially to blame. Black people are partly to blame also. It is never one group that is totally to blame for the problems that exist.

Q. *How can you equate community control of a school district in a large city with community control of a suburban district when it is a fact that suburban families pay the taxes necessary for the operation of their schools?*

A. On this matter of taxes, it would be interesting to find out how much taxes black people pay in the United States and the kind of services they get in return. We do not get any reduction on taxes. The money goes around the world, rebuilding France and Germany and other war-torn countries while we still fight to get a little handout on welfare. This is our money. Poor people are paying taxes. When you spend a dollar, five cents of that goes to taxes. I do not care how poor you are. When you buy a gallon of gasoline, eleven to twelve cents of it goes to taxes. When we ask for a little of it back, we are told we can not have it. They are sending it to the moon. They are sending it everywhere else.

Q. *How can the situation in the schools be remedied?*

A. There has to be more faith in the black man on the part of the white man in America. Blacks have been having faith for three hundred years. That is all we have had—faith. We have been believing in whites from slavery right up. We have had faith in them and we still do. We have been looking to whites to educate our children, looking to them for all sorts of things. We have had faith in whites and have not lost that faith, but now you have got to have faith in us. That means, if a black community wants to run its schools and a white man wants to come and work in them, he does not come on his own terms and dictate to that community, as was done in Ocean Hill-Brownsville. That does not work. We are not going to accept it. It is un-American and we are American enough to say "NO!" to it. There has to be more faith in the black man. The less faith the white people have, the more furious blacks get. I am really grappling for a solution to the problem because for a long time I thought integration was going to do it, but it is not. Integration was killing us. Now if the only resort is some other kind of nationalism, it has to be sought out. If integration will not work, we just cannot go on trusting that integration is going to work. The white man has the power to make integration work. We do not have the power and it has not yet been demonstrated whether the black man can make integration work. I would say in Ocean Hill-Brownsville that we had more integration than one has in white districts. We brought in a Puerto Rican and made him the principal of a school, the first Puerto Rican principal in New York City. We brought in a Chinese principal—the first in the history of education in the United States. We brought in white principals. We did not say a thing about integration. The safest place even during the strikes was at Ocean Hill-

Brownsville where white people could come and get portions of a street in which to picket, in a black community and get police protection to do it. When I and a small group went down to Canarsie, a white area, just to walk in front of Canarsie High School, the police would not allow us to use the sidewalk. They put us on the curb. It was our right to use the sidewalk, but the policemen allowed the picketers to monopolize the sidewalk and ushered us to the curb, while in Ocean Hill, white picketers had police protection while occupying a whole street. You had more than 3,000 policemen in Ocean Hill-Brownsville at one time, in that little community. When the people saw all those policemen out there they just concluded that the Governing Board must be doing something right, and it brought them to our side.

8

Teacher Unionism and Education

ALBERT SHANKER

What are teacher unions all across the country fighting for, and why is it that teachers are organizing? What are the major urban educational problems to which teacher unions, particularly the UFT in New York City, have devoted their energies? What are the major problems that are before us in urban education and what role can teacher unions play in solving these problems?

If one looks at teacher slogans, newspapers, and negotiated contracts, one finds three major areas of concern common to teachers all across the country. These three areas—economics, professionalism, and the civil rights of teachers—are common to educators in New York, Washington, D.C., Chicago, Philadelphia, and other urban centers.

It should be said that this movement toward teacher organizations is quite recent. It was only in November 1960 that teachers in New York City went out on their first strike, a strike to win collective bargaining rights. Thus, until November 1960, and indeed beyond that to December 1961, when the UFT was elected collective bargaining agent in New York City, there was not a single teacher organization anywhere in the United States that had exclusive collective bargaining recognition. No teacher organization anywhere in the United States had the right to sit down and enter into negotiations leading to a written agreement with a board of education.

The whole problem of teacher power, teacher unionism, teachers' collective bargaining is something that is recent. Yet, within this very short period of time, it has spread across the country. About one-third of the states in the United States now have laws requiring boards of education to enter into negotiations with teachers, to recognize them and to have written agreements with them. The organization of teachers into a collective bargaining type of organization, which in other words is a union, whether it be affiliated with the AFL-CIO or the NEA, is new and spreading rapidly. Within the next five years the majority of states in the United States will require such negotiations.

Economics is the first of the three areas of common concern to teachers which I will discuss. I start with it deliberately because for many years teachers were afraid to express their concerns with their own well being and the well being of their families. Somehow, teachers alone, among all groups of employees, have been brainwashed into believing that if they expressed a concern with making more money so that they could have a nicer home or a second car and all the other necessary and unnecessary things that other people in our society indulge, that somehow this concern with money would be an indication that they were not really interested in their subject matter and not really interested in their pupils. It would show that they were interested in money rather than in a concern for service.

This concept that there is a conflict between one's concern with supporting one's family at a proper level and one's concern with one's life work exists in no other profession. People have not assumed that because a doctor makes a great deal of money, this conflicts with his concern for his patient. As a matter of fact, most people would not dare go to a doctor who earns the kind of money a teacher earns for fear that something is wrong with the doctor. In a society where money and material things are valued so highly, I am rather surprised that parents have entrusted their children for so long to teachers who exhibited such a lack of concern for material gain. Certainly, this lack of concern is a great abnormality.

The first part of this economic area deals with salary, pensions and welfare benefits. It does, however, go beyond the immediate "cash in the pocket." The economic sphere includes such things as the right of the teacher to have a duty-free lunch period and the notion that teaching is a rather exacting type of work which is very difficult to do from 8:30 A.M. until 3 or 3:30 P.M. without professional preparation periods, or free periods. I might say this concept of free periods is one which raises a great deal of public opposition. If a parent walks through a school and sees a teachers' room with a group of teachers relaxing, smoking, reading the newspaper, playing cards or marking papers, a fantastic amount of resentment wells up. The idea that a teacher, who works a short year and a short day, is not with the children and not teaching every minute of the day disturbs parents. Yet, that same parent, when she has to spend a day home with her own three children, says to her husband when he comes home, "I can't stand it any more! Take them off my hands! I'm going to the movies or the hairdresser." The very same mother who finds it almost impossible to take care of her own three youngsters in the rather free atmosphere of a home, where there are many rooms and a television set and where there is no requirement that the children learn anything, begrudges a teacher who has to take care of thirty or more children for an entire day forty-five minutes during that day for relaxation.

In addition to the money aspect, welfare items, pension, a duty-free lunch period, and relaxation during the day, one of the greatest concerns of teachers throughout the country deals with replacing, by a method of fair play and objectivity, the system of politics and patronage that exists within almost every school system and every school building. I am referring to the fact that a teacher who stands up at a faculty conference and criticizes the principal finds that his chances of getting the difficult classes, year after year, are considerably enhanced. I am also saying that a teacher who sits around the teachers' room and listens to the complaints of other teachers and carries them back to the principal, has a good chance of getting administrative assignments and relief from difficult assignments. Within every school and every school system there is a system of petty rewards and petty punishments. Those who support the administration are encouraged and their lives are made easier than the lives of those teachers who criticize the administration even mildly. In some cases teachers' statements, even when not given as criticism but taken as such, often result in the teachers' receiving various patrol assignments, the most difficult classes, and the oldest set of books. Within each school two types of careers are possible. One can be rather pleasant, the other quite miserable, depending upon the course the administration takes in handing out the welcomed assignments and the onerous chores.

One of the things that teachers are asking is that a set of qualifications be promulgated for the desirable jobs within schools throughout the country. There should be an objective way for teachers to qualify. Qualifications should be posted, and teachers should be given an equal opportunity to apply for the positions. When a number of teachers are found to be equally well qualified for a particular position, there ought to be some objective means of selection (such as, giving each person a chance for the job, or drawing lots). The power to make someone happy or the power to make someone miserable on the basis of that choice should not lie in the hands of an individual principal. Similarly, if there are horribly unpleasant tasks within the school which must be performed by teachers, then everyone ought to have an opportunity to do his share for the school before anyone is required to do it a second, or a third, time. Unpleasant tasks ought to be rotated.

A second aspect of economic concern is the question of nonprofessional assignments for teachers. One of the major thrusts within the economic area has been the demand to relieve teachers of the many nonprofessional chores with which they have been burdened. These chores fall within two separate categories; one being clerical functions and the other being the police types of functions. I would say that a third type of function, which we have tried to eliminate and which we feel is really nonprofessional, consists of the administrative tasks within schools which teachers are asked to perform. We do not believe that the administrative chores of the schools necessarily have to be done by teachers. If you place competent administrators without education backgrounds in administrative positions in school systems, administrative chores will be more competently and more quickly performed. In addition, the expertise of educators will not be wasted.

Third on this economic list is the notion of a grievance procedure. If an individual is constantly being discriminated against, or if the written agreement which the teachers enter into with the Board of Education is violated, there must be some recourse for the teacher. Eventually an arbitrator or a judge who is not related to the system will make the final determination as to whether the teacher who feels aggrieved is right or wrong. The existence of grievance machinery outside the school system is extremely important.

In the days before collective bargaining if a principal did something supposedly unfair, and a teacher complained, the principal, of course, asserted that he was absolutely right. At each level of the school system, there was a tendency to constantly support the colleague who made the decision, even when they thought it was wrong. If the district superintendent or the superintendent of schools publicly said that a principal was wrong, it would have undermined that principal's authority within his school. The superintendent might privately call the principal aside and say, "I think that was pretty stupid. If I were you, I wouldn't do it. I won't back you up if you do this again, but this time I'm going to save you." This army-like tendency of each level to back up the next level is no longer possible, because the grievance ends up outside each level of the decision-making process. Grievance procedure tends to make principals more careful because they feel the embarrassment of having some outside arbitrator coming in and saying, "Not only is the principal wrong but all these people up and down the line who backed him are wrong."

Of course, these aspects do not constitute the entire economic package. I have discussed some of the significant and universal aspects of teacher-union contracts throughout the country. Those who have never seen a comprehensive collective bargaining agreement should be aware that, in addition to these broad areas, there are many small items concerning teachers of the home-bound and teachers of children of retarded mental development. Special working conditions in the elementary schools, the junior high schools, and the vocational schools are detailed. Virtually anything that teachers are bothered with and discuss in the lunch room, eventually finds its way into a contract.

A second area of concern to teachers is the professional area. The word "professional" must be used carefully. It is a word that has been stood on its head by educators. The word "professional," as used by most educators means "Be sure to obey orders." "Don't rock the boat." "Don't criticize anybody." I remember that when I started teaching, there were only a few men in my school, and the tradition had been that on snow days they would all go down and patrol the block to see that the students did not throw snowballs at each other. This was known as snow patrol, and somehow it was considered a very unlady-like activity. That particular year the number of men on the faculty increased from three to six, so at the first faculty conference one of the teachers raised his hand and asked, "Now that we have six men on the faculty instead of three, can't we have our lunch period and have three men go out during the first snowfall and have the other three be on duty during the second snowfall? Can't we rotate this?" The principal stood up and said, "I think that's very unprofessional." The teacher was not obeying orders. He was questioning the administration. I could repeat a number of other cases where throughout my career in the school system the word "professional" was used in a very strange manner. The implication was clear that a professional in the school system is about the closest thing to a dead person you can possibly imagine. He is capable of locomotion, but not much else.

A professional is not a meekly obedient person who follows orders unthinkingly. A professional person has a high degree of decision-making power within the field in which he is an expert. He is relatively unsupervised after he goes through an initial training period. He functions in a self-directed manner. You would not find, for instance, a surgeon walking into an operating room of his hospital and then having the chief administrator of the operating room walking in and directing the surgeon, "Cut a little to the left." or "Cut a little to the right." It is not that the chief administrator is not also a professional; he is. He is an expert in buying food, hiring nurses, and scheduling operations so that not too many operations are being performed simultaneously. As a matter of fact, the surgeon could not be successful unless the chief administrator of the hospital was also successful in his profession, in terms of administratively running the hospital.

Unfortunately, in the field of teaching, we are not in a very high professional state. The teachers are not treated as people who have a high degree of expertise in a particular area. They are constantly watched. They are subject to the rules and regulations of the administrators. A rather outstanding and interesting example of this occurred not very long ago. About ten years ago there was a teacher at Mt. Kisco, New York, not a member of the union, who was head of a department in the Fox Land High School. His personnel folder contained many letters saying that he was a fine teacher. One day he came back from his summer vacation and found that there was a new principal in his school who called the entire faculty together and made a speech which went something like this: "Very happy to have all of you back. I know that this is a very fine staff and you are all professionals. The mark of a professional is that he plans ahead, so I want each and every one of you to bring in, this coming Monday, the first day of school, a complete period-by-period lesson plan for the entire year in advance, so that we can be ahead of all the other districts in this country."

Of course, all the other teachers in the school were "professional" and they went home over the weekend and came in with the big volume of lesson plans. What happened then was that the principal initialed them and gave each of the teachers a big gold star or whatever it is that one gets when one submits a nice plan book.

But James Wally was not like that. He went into the principal's office very disturbed. He said that he could do as the others had done, but it would be sheer hypocrisy. He knew very well that he would not be following those plans period-by-period after a few weeks and certainly not after a year. Instead, he volunteered to submit a detailed daily or weekly plan. He volunteered to submit monthly plans which would be a general overview of what he wanted to accomplish. He would even submit an actual plan describing the outcomes he expected, the text he expected to use, and how he would handle the difficulties that he expected to encounter. The principal of the school said "No!" and he was ordered to come in with the plan book a year in advance. When he did not do so, he was fired.

Here we have a rather crucial distinction. A professional, you will remember, is a person who is an expert, and you fire an expert if he is not really expert in his area. But practically no teachers are ever fired for incompetence. They are fired, as James Wally was, for insubordination. Insubordination, however, is not a professional concept; it is a military concept. It is a concept which says, "You are a buck private, and your sergeant says you follow the sergeant's orders because he has more stripes than you have." There is no question as to whether he is more competent, as to whether he is right, as to whether he is wrong. The sergeant has the right to give orders to the private. The private must obey.

I submit that the structure of most of our school systems today is not a professional one. In a professional structure the teacher has an area of expertise in which he is given a great degree of freedom to operate, regardless of the orders of the principal, superintendent, department chairman, or assistant principal. If he fails to demonstrate competency in this area, he should be made responsible for his failures, but he should be fired for proven incompetence, not for insubordination.

Let me point out a second aspect of this antiprofessionalism within school systems. Throughout most of the country the process by which one becomes a principal or a superintendent is by being a coach of a football or basketball team, and when the team happens to have a streak of bad luck and keeps losing, a new coach is needed. The way to remove the present coach is to make him an administrator. He is made a superintendent or principal. On a national basis, an extremely disproportionate number of coaches in administrative positions can be found. Once that coach becomes the principal of a particular school, under the military system, he feels that it is perfectly within his province to walk into the room of the French teacher, the math teacher, the cooking teacher, or the industrial arts teacher, to sit at the rear of their rooms and tell them what they are doing wrong in their particular fields. Of course, this is a gross violation of the notion of professionalism in which, if there is supervision and evaluation, it is not on the basis that somebody happened to achieve a certain rank, but is based on the supervisor's having superior competence in a particular field.

What is now becoming more and more of an issue is the demand on the part of teachers that they be considered professional, which means that they be free from the dictates of administrators, except insofar as administrators and supervisors actually have greater competence in their particular fields. There is a reason why it is becoming a rather popular view. In urban areas, fifteen years ago, there was a tremendous educational gap between the teacher and principal. At one time, the typical teacher in New York City was a graduate of a training school with perhaps two years of education, and the principal was at least a college graduate and held a master's degree. Therefore, the teacher looked up to the principal as someone who had more years of education. This is no longer true in most of our schools. Quite a few teachers have actually had more education in their own fields than the principal has had. A principal may have had nine or twelve credits in administration, but he has had much less training than I have had in mathematics or the teaching of mathematics. Therefore, there is less willingness on the part of teachers to accept authority.

The third area of concern to teachers deals with civil rights, that is, the right of a teacher to engage in the same normal activities as any other citizen in the community. It is still true that in many parts of the country a teacher is not free to have a beer at the local bar because somehow there is an image of his morality being apart and different from that of anyone else. If anyone else goes into the bar, it is because he wants a beer. If a teacher goes in, however, some student may find out that he drinks beer and this would seriously impair the morals of the youngster. There still exists the notion that a community has the right to control the personal activities of teachers. This attitude is manifested in many communities throughout this country, and of course, recently figured in the Ocean Hill-Brownsville dispute where the most serious charge against the teachers was that they had criticized the local governing board.

To summarize: there are three areas of common concern to teachers across the country. The first is economic, dealing with money, relief from nonteaching chores, reduction of teaching load, the equitable distribution of the good jobs and the difficult jobs within the school, and a grievance procedure. The second area is the professional area, which essentially deals with the right of a teacher to practice what he is expert in, relatively free from supervision, except on the part of those who have superior expertise in that particular field. The third is the area of civil and political rights which guarantees free speech, the ability to engage in political activity in a particular community, and the freedom to live the kind of life he wishes, just as all other members of the community have the freedom to live as they wish.

These three areas also involve urban problems. In the first place, the strength of teacher unions is generally in urban areas. The National Education Association, which is one nationwide teacher organization, is primarily a rural and suburban organization. The American Federation of Teachers is primarily an urban organization which represents teachers not only in New York City but also in Chicago, Cleveland, Detroit, Philadelphia, Baltimore, Washington, D.C., and Boston. The National Education Association now represents, as far as big cities are concerned, only one large city—Milwaukee.

There is a reason for this difference in membership. Generally, teachers are more likely to speak and organize in large cosmopolitan areas than they are in small towns. In small towns, if you join a controversial organization, the community is likely to get rid of you or make life so difficult you cannot stay. This is generally not true in big cities. Of course, most big cities have a large union movement and teachers, in trying to enhance their own power, generally wish to ally themselves with other groups in the city which have a substantial amount of power. Therefore, teachers have generally chosen to ally themselves with this powerful group within the large cities.

Let me very briefly talk about some of the major problems which face the UFT and other local unions, and which have become part of the main thrust of negotiations. In the first place, one of the major concerns has been the reduction of class size. Those of you who have been teaching only a few years may find it impossible to believe that in 1963, 25 percent of the high school classes had forty-five or forty-six pupils in a class. The maximum is now down to thirty-three. It may seem hard to believe that in 1963, 25 percent of the elementary school classes in New York City had forty children in them. Class size has been a major area of concern, and I put this under the category of urban problems because it is generally agreed that in order for education to be more effective, we need greater individualization of instruction. It is easier to reach each child in a class of twenty children than in a class where there are forty or forty-six. It does not mean it is impossible to teach with forty-six—it has been done—and I know there is some controversy about whether small classes are necessarily an advantage. However, if you look at how Governor Rockefeller (or anybody else with any money) reacts when his children fall behind a little, you would find that they go out and hire individual tutors. They know what to do. I can assure you that if the children of the people who sit around arguing about whether small class size really means anything, fell behind in their studies, and if they had the money, they would not argue about the philosophical niceties of smaller class size. They would go out and put those children in a one-to-one relationship.

Our second problem has been the very great problem of teacher turnover, which is related to the question of teacher training. Teachers should not be permitted to hold permanent licenses without having a very expensive on-the-job training program similar to a doctor's internship. Yet, up to now it was really impossible to do that because of the high staff turnover. In New York City, until recently, between six to nine thousand new teachers were needed each year.

What does it take to train six thousand new teachers? The beginning teacher should not be teaching full time. She should probably be teaching half time so that she can concentrate on doing a great deal of planning and on working with more experienced teachers in the school. That means that instead of hiring six thousand new teachers, each of whom is only going to teach half the time, you have to hire twelve thousand in order to cover the same number of classes. That is very expensive. Then, if you are also going to free some experienced teachers in a school to work with the inexperienced ones, you have to "cover them" for the period of time when they are out of the classroom. This becomes almost impossible. Let me add one other complicating factor—what happens after you train these teachers? Up to now, teachers have remained in the school system for an average of three years. This means that they remain in teaching just long enough to experiment at the expense of the children. Then they leave and do not come back. Only a very small proportion of teachers remain.

The recent contract which the UFT (in New York City) negotiated, however, in which teachers reach a maximum of $16,000 after eight years and where they move up at the rate of $1,700 a year has already had a fantastic effect. The Teachers' Retirement Board now has lines of people waiting to withdraw their retirement papers. Administrators from Long Island, Rockland County and Westchester County report that their districts were about to hire many New York City teachers, assistant principals and chairmen. These people have now decided to remain in New York City because they cannot afford to leave. Graduate education majors may have to wait another six months or a year for a job. There will be a huge lineup of thousands of teachers waiting to come into the system. What will happen as a result of this is that there is going to be very little turnover. There is going to be a stable teaching staff and it is going to be possible to train and retrain teachers because we will know that the teachers we have today are not leaving this year or the year after but are staying for ten or fifteen years.

Through the union's contract, we have solved a number of other problems which have plagued most cities. The transfer plan in our contract effectively limits the right of teachers to get out of the schools that they are in. In most cases, it takes about ten years before you can transfer. Before collective bargaining, it used to be possible for a teacher, after three years, to transfer to another school. Teachers were practically on roller skates within a school system. Annually, there used to be four thousand transfers of regular teachers alone. Now there are perhaps eight hundred.

What have we accomplished through this slowing-down process? In the first place, the teacher with seniority has the right to transfer into a given school free from any selective process by the principal and anybody else who may want to either reward or punish somebody. But even more important, we now have the same percentage of regular and substitute teachers in ghetto schools and in non-ghetto schools. In other words, what the federal government has said about Chicago—that the ghetto schools all have substitute teachers who remain about six months and then get out to move on to another job—cannot be said of New York City because of the plan which has severely restricted the movement of teachers.

I cannot go through this whole list, but I will conclude on this note. There has been much written recently—including the Coleman Report, Pat Sexton's book relating poverty and education, some of the works of Christopher Jencks, and quite a few others—essentially saying that the amount of impact that formal schooling has on children is much more limited than what we had thought up to now. It is not possible for a school to overcome all of the problems which children bring with them. That does not mean that schools cannot do anything. If I believed that, I would be in favor of closing them down and doing something else with the money saved. Schools can do more than they are doing now, and it is not enough for us to sit back and say "Children bring so many problems with them that we're all excused. We can't do anything." That would be a horrible attitude and position to take, but what can be done is much more limited than what we had thought up to now.

If it is true that the ability of a child to function educationally is to some extent dependent upon how much money his parents make; what kind of a house he lives in, whether it is rat infested and sweltering in the summer and freezing in the winter, or whether it is a fairly decent place; whether he comes to school with food in his stomach; whether he is subject to a whole system of discrimination; whether there is a feeling of relative freedom in terms of opportunity, then it is not enough for teachers to sit back and say, "I will use a better reader. I will use a little more planning. I will work a little harder tomorrow in school . . ." and to forget about all these other factors in a child's life which are preventing him from responding to the things which we are doing in the classroom.

In other words, let us assume that a mother comes in from across the street and wants to know why her child is not doing as well as other children and the teacher says, "Well, I can't help it because you live in the slums, you have a broken home, your child does not get breakfast in the morning, you have rats and leaky ceilings over there. How do you expect me to teach your child?" One of these days that parent is going to turn around to the teacher and say, "Do you think I want to live in that place? What have you ever done to help me and other people like me get decent housing and jobs and live in a world where we don't have to be discriminated against constantly in everything that we do?" As illustrated here, the teacher is being extremely narrow and in many ways self-defeating if he or she concentrates his efforts only on the school, classroom and curriculum.

Part of the educational problem has to be resolved in the political sphere. It is for this reason that the unionization of teachers is so important. We cannot get jobs, eliminate discrimination, get decent housing, and move toward the concept of a guaranteed annual income, without a tremendous governmental commitment. That commitment will come only if many groups work together. Black groups in this country are not numerous enough or strong enough to bring that about by themselves. Concerned people, like the ones registered for courses in urban education, are not strong enough to bring that about by themselves. Labor unions are not strong enough to bring it about by themselves. It is necessary within a democratic society to build a coalition, a partnership of political forces, of groups that do not necessarily love each other on all issues but agree on these issues. One of the most significant factors of the unionization of teachers in large cities is that it will, within a few years, provide a large, mass organization of one million teachers, all of them college graduates. When this organization becomes politically activated it will start moving, as other unions in the past have moved, toward an alliance with civil rights groups, labor unions, and liberal forces throughout the country to bring about some of the necessary social changes which will result in greater social impact than what we ourselves can bring about within schools.

9

Education and the
Puerto Rican Child

JOSEPH MONSERRAT

The quality of the education received by the Puerto Rican child in a city such as New York, or in any of the other 200 cities where Puerto Rican children reside, will depend upon the success of the schools in teaching all of the children in urban school systems. By almost any measurement, the Puerto Rican student is doing very poorly in school. If we examine drop-out percentages, we find that the rate Puerto Rican children leave school is higher than that of any other ethnic group. If we define success in high schools as the acquisition of an academic diploma, again, the Puerto Rican child compares poorly. In New York City, fewer than 10 percent of the Puerto Rican students who enter high school graduate with either an academic or a commercial diploma. Some will graduate with a certificate of attendance, called a general diploma. Most, however, quit school prior to graduation without possessing marketable skills.

One requirement necessary for successfully educating any

group of children is an understanding of the nature of the "reality" which confronts that particular group. The reality of the problem facing Puerto Ricans in New York, or any other city in the country, has nothing to do with the fact that Puerto Ricans come from a different culture and speak a different language. That is not the problem. The reality is that if we look at the history of the United States, we see that it is marked by constant migration and immigration. Yet, throughout that history, the United States never welcomed anybody, at any time, with open arms. We teach children, and were taught ourselves, that the founding fathers came in search of religious and political liberty, and most teachers put a period there. Unfortunately, we cannot put a period there. The most we can do is put a semicolon or a dash and add the words "for themselves—it was not extended to others."

In contemporary America we are still confronted with a continuation of this philosophy. No migrant group is welcomed with open arms, regardless of what the ethnic majority might be in the particular area. The history of America has been a constant effort by new groups to become equal to the rest of society. If you were not a member of the Congregational Church in Massachusetts, you did not vote. Then there was the city of Salem. If you did not believe in the religion of its rulers, you were a heretic and treated accordingly. In order to understand the failure of our schools today, we must realize that education does not relate to reality as the Puerto Rican child perceives it. Our schools are a reflection of the national social setting: a setting which is characterized by the struggle of ethnic groups to achieve the "American dream." Not only has the United States failed to welcome newcomers at any time in its history, but it has never succeeded in healing the wounds created by the friction of the first generation of immigrant groups. All immigrant groups have had the same basic problems. Because these problems have never been resolved, each migrant group has had the problems passed on to it.

For example, Lincoln Steffens and Jacob Riis carefully documented the slum conditions of the lower East Side at the turn of the century. Yet, the buildings which they classified as slums then are still standing today. The people who lived on the East Side at that time—the Puerto Ricans of their day—did not resolve the problems of the lower East Side. They moved away; the problems remained. New people have moved in and are faced with the same problems. Now, however, instead of speaking Russian, Polish or Yiddish, they speak Spanish. The Puerto Ricans did not create the slums of the East Side, nor any other slums in New York. They merely moved into existing slums and became the victims of these slums. This illustrates a repetitive historical process in which the newcomer is the victim of the existing problems.

One of the reasons America has not resolved these chronic problems is that it sought the solution in the newcomer and not in the social structure. Consequently, as the newcomer moved up the scale and away from the problem, the problem was thought to be solved. For example, the presence of non-English-speaking children in the New York City school system is as old as the school system itself. In terms of numbers, the system had to cope with much larger non-English-speaking groups in the past. The Puerto Rican migration to the mainland is one of the smallest ever to take place. There are approximately one million and a half Puerto Ricans in the fifty states. In the history of immigration to this country, there were periods in which one million people migrated to this country in a single year. There are only about four million Puerto Ricans in the world, and if they all came here to the United States they would still constitute a smaller group than any of the major groups that preceded them.

The real problem is that between the immigration laws of 1921 and the aftermath of World War II, when the Puerto Rican migration grew, little was done to solve the problems of immigrant groups, or even to understand their problems.

Before educators can begin to cope with this problem, they must understand its nature. I cannot accept the thesis that Puerto Ricans cannot be educated. The function of teachers and the educational establishment is to teach children. When children do not learn, education's failures cannot be excused by blaming the larger society. If a teacher cannot successfully teach children, whoever they may be, he should not be in education. The failures of the educational establishment are creating a dangerous vacuum which may be filled by a variety of nonprofessional groups, many of which will wage war on the professionals.

The United States is one of the few countries in the world where a man can consider himself educated and yet speak only one language. This is so despite the fact that we are a nation which has received large numbers of people who have spoken all of the world's modern languages. Why then are we monolingual? Walt Whitman said, "This is not a nation, but a teeming nation of nations." Thus, some people said we needed one language to bind us and to overcome the problems posed by our country's great size and ethnic diversity. I disagree with this argument. I believe that the reason we are a monolingual nation is because to be different in the United States has meant to be "less than," to be inferior. The Constitution, however, does not state that English should be the official national language. The fact is that the first Puerto Rican migrant to the United States was probably Ponce de León, the first governor of Puerto Rico, who in 1513 discovered what today is the state of Florida. We should also remember that when the Pilgrims landed on a rock, an Indian probably looked out from behind a tree and said, "Ugh! Foreigners!" The founding fathers of America could have been greeted in Spanish, French, or Dutch, if they had landed on other parts of the North American coast.

English did not have to be our national language. We forget that there is a part of this country which by treaty became bilingual. The Treaty of Guadalupe Hidalgo, which ended the Mexican War, gave one hundred thousand former citizens of Mexico the right to retain their culture, language, religion and to become United States citizens within one year if they stayed in the territory we now know as the state of New Mexico. New Mexico is a bilingual state in which both Spanish and English are official languages. So, English need not always be the unifying element, particularly in New York and some other eastern seaboard cities.

Unfortunately, this problem of language and cultural identity has never been resolved. And this is the problem that Puerto Rican youth faces. They have the same options that most Americans had before them. Which ones they choose, and which ones are forced on them will reflect, to some degree, the success or failure of our educational system.

In order to fit the American stereotype many newcomers have given up the language, culture, values, religion, and even the names of their parents. One of the problems of contemporary urban education is the lack of knowledge and awareness on the part of teachers of their own immediate past. Because they belonged to the immigrant groups of yesterday, they reject the Puerto Ricans today who are an uncomfortable reflection of an earlier, less prestigous identity. Too many of us do not want to look in the mirror. In the haste to run away, and perhaps in the shame of having had to run away, we do not want to see somebody who is trying to overcome the same filth, poor housing, inadequate education, and meagre vocational opportunities which had confronted us.

These are the problems which make it difficult to successfully educate the Puerto Rican student. This is part of the reality he faces. He is not welcome in the community because he is a stranger in the country—although he is a born citizen, as was his father before him. He is a foreigner in his own country because too many Americans cannot understand that you can be an American without speaking English.

Puerto Ricans can be born in Puerto Rico and never learn a word of English but still function perfectly as American citizens. Unfortunately, too many Americans cannot accept this emotionally. Intellectually they can understand that Puerto Ricans are citizens, but they cannot accept the fact that Puerto Ricans can forego going through the process of getting citizenship papers. When this emotional attitude steps into education —and it does—the Puerto Rican child is faced with an enormous problem, not of his making, but which nevertheless affects him greatly.

Americans must understand that most Puerto Ricans have lived in the continental United States less than twenty years. Thus, when one compares them to previous immigrant groups, we immediately label columns: black, Puerto Ricans and "others"; and then we pretend that we are measuring equal groups. This is unfair. If you want to measure Puerto Ricans as a group by any other group in the past, the comparison should be of the situation when that group had been here only twenty years. Do not measure them against groups that have had two or three generations in this country. This is unfair and misleading. The Puerto Rican community as such does not yet have a second generation native to this country. Eighty-five percent of the Puerto Rican youngsters born in the United States are fourteen years of age or younger. We do not have a large second generation of Puerto Ricans twenty-one years or older, or large numbers who have been able to go through schools because they have not had enough time to do so. Given the time, the Puerto Rican will be able to match the contributions and successes of previous immigrant groups to the United States.

Teachers of Puerto Rican children should remember that there are at least three major identifiable groups within the Puerto Rican community. The first generation Puerto Rican is the person born in Puerto Rico, raised in Puerto Rico, educated in Puerto Rico, who then migrated to the United States.

When he migrated, he brought with him the value system of the area of Puerto Rico from which he came. Actually, the first generation Puerto Ricans came from different Puerto Ricos, because the Puerto Rican from Ponce, which is in the middle of the Island, is different from the Puerto Rican from the slums of El Fangito in San Juan. They are two different parts of Puerto Rico, and his reaction to the mainland is going to be based on the reality he knew on the Island.

This is similar to what an American experiences when he goes to Europe and proceeds to measure everything by U.S. standards. I have heard people who returned from Europe say, "Do you know that they don't even toast their bread over there! Can you imagine!" I must ask, "What the devil did you go there for?" Others say, "In Spain they have dinner at 10:00 P.M., and I go to bed at 10:00 P.M." "If you go to bed at 10:00 P.M., then stay home!" But Americans go over there and decide to impose their values on others, absolutely sure that those values are superior. We are doing this now to Puerto Ricans. We tell Puerto Ricans "Look, forget your language, forget your values, depersonalize yourself. Become something you are not." Within that vacuum, we begin to educate their children. This is idiocy. Yet, this is what we do, and because the Puerto Rican cannot succeed he often quits school. I do not care who the newcomer is, these realities exist because of the traumatic factor of change.

The second group of Puerto Ricans is the "bridge" generation. Born in Puerto Rico, they received some of their education in Puerto Rico, but they migrated to the mainland at an early age and continued their education and growing-up process here. This group has the strength of knowing what it is to be a Puerto Rican in Puerto Rico, as well as the added factor of knowing more about the reality here than does the first generation.

The third group is the main one that teachers will be dealing with: the second generation youngster born here of Puerto

Rican parents. It is important to know more about this group. In the first place, we must understand that the Puerto Rican child born in New York is not Puerto Rican in the same sense as his cousin who is actually living in Puerto Rico. He cannot be: he is reacting to stimuli around him which are totally different from the stimuli to which his cousin is reacting in Puerto Rico. In Puerto Rico a child is in schools where he is accepted. In Puerto Rico he is part of the group. Here he is a minority. His father and older brother do not quite understand this minority status, because in Puerto Rico the only minority groups that exist are unsuccessful political parties. Puerto Rico does not have minorities. They have no need to use that nomenclature.

On the mainland, however, the father begins to see something happen to his child because of the different situation which faces his child. The reality here is that the child is not Puerto Rican, but neither is he an "American." The Puerto Rican child is now in a state of limbo, being neither fish nor fowl.

The parents of this child gave him the same love that all parents give their children. When he was born his parents decided that they wanted to educate him, they wanted to toilet train him and and show him how to eat, to teach him manners and communicate with him. They also did something that some people think was very detrimental to the child. They taught him Spanish. They wanted to speak with their child, and since Spanish was the language they knew, that was the language they used. The parents may now know English but they felt that if their child was to know a language other than English they had better teach him at home, because in school he would learn English. Of course, if the child attends a secondary school where he is taught Spanish as a foreign language, his teachers would want him to be able to speak it and understand it as well as he did when he entered first grade.

But we do not want him to speak it and understand it when he enters the first grade.

The Puerto Rican child brings to school an asset which has now been turned into a liability. We do not see it as an asset. We do not believe that speaking Spanish is important. Of course, his parents, who taught him how to speak Spanish, are to blame. The teacher says it was a mistake and most Puerto Ricans believe that teachers are never wrong. The teacher is the only person in the child's life who is always right. She knows all the answers. She grades him every day and has immense power. If the teacher said so, the child will tell his mother, "Oh no! Miss Smith said this. . . ." And the youngster will argue about it with Mama. Thus, if the teacher says, "You should not speak Spanish," how does a child feel about parents who taught him the language. Then, if a nutritionist should come along and say, "Tell your mother not to give you rice and beans," the child goes home and says, "Hey, Ma, roast beef and mashed potatoes."

In addition, if the Puerto Rican child is led to believe that all the ills of the city exist because he migrated there, he may withdraw into a self-protective shell with his own group and do nothing but speak in Spanish. Others may go to the other extreme and reject everything that is Spanish, including their parents, and try to become "all American." There are others who are caught in the middle and who, as a result, have all kinds of psychological problems. There is nothing new about this. It is the exact historical process that all immigrant groups have gone through.

Part of the problem is that what has happened to others before is happening now to these youngsters. Another part of the problem is that we hear people say, as a justification, "Well, that happened to us too," as if the fact that "it happened to us" is a valid reason for its happening now to other children. It should never have happened before. It was as wrong then as it is now. In fact, it may even be less defensible now because America has had experience with earlier immigrants. But we rationalize injustice and we approve of it because we do not have the gumption to fight injustice. I think it is only within this framework that one can begin to understand some of the problems involved in the education of the Puerto Rican child. That is why I say that many of the issues in education are not educational issues in the narrow sense of the word.

Another problem facing Puerto Rican youngsters is the nature of their race. Puerto Ricans are difficult to categorize racially. They are black, white, and mixed. I am not saying that there are no color problems in Puerto Rico, but I say emphatically that these problems have no relationship to those on the mainland. The conditioning of the people is different. They do not talk about a minority group. Youngsters do not know the meaning of a minority group based on race. Where schools are 100 percent Puerto Rican, they are not segregated. On the mainland, however, this colored Puerto Rican child enters a school where, because of the nature of the society, he is labeled inferior. His color has nothing to do with his ability, but it will exert a critical influence on the way his teacher sees him and thus effect his educational achievements. The reality as it exists in Puerto Rico is quite different from that in the United States.

The confused reaction of parents to this situation is something that must be understood. I believe that the first generation and the bridge generation have the strength to know what it is to be a Puerto Rican in Puerto Rico, which means they have added strength in helping them adjust to their present situation. They do not have the psychosis or know the syndrome of what it is to be a minority group member. They were not raised or conditioned for minority group status in Puerto Rico. But their children, who are born here, face the reality of the city ghetto. They do not know what it is not to be a member of the minority group because they are born into that minority.

The child's reality resembles the reality not of his father and mother, who were raised in Puerto Rico, but the reality of other children raised in the ghetto. Because of this, he can identify more easily, for example, with his black brother than can his mother and father. This problem will grow with the youngsters who are born here, as they grow in number and age.

There is one experience that some Puerto Rican youngsters have which should be used for educational purposes and that is Puerto Rico itself. The youngsters frequently return to Puerto Rico and see average citizens in every walk of life. They see the skilled construction worker, the mason, the carpenter, the engineer, the architect, the capitalist and the banker, all of whom contribute to the construction of a building. They learn that, in Puerto Rico, if someone is arrested, the policeman is a Puerto Rican and the lawyer is a Puerto Rican. In court, the attorney for the prosecution is a Puerto Rican; the judge, a Puerto Rican; the jury, Puerto Rican. In the jails, the warden is Puerto Rican; the parole board is Puerto Rican. On the Island, you do not have to make up success stories to prove to the Puerto Rican child that he, too, can succeed. Puerto Rico is a reality and it has a reflection in the United States. It will have a continuing reality in the life of the Puerto Rican in New York and in the other cities in which he resides.

10

Militancy and Violence: A Challenge to Urban Secondary Schools

SHELDON MARCUS and PHILIP D. VAIRO

Many people are quite concerned with student violence on college campuses. Yet, violence in the high schools of the United States is a more frequent phenomenon than violence on college campuses. Columbia University's Center for Research and Education on American Liberties disclosed recently that there were 239 nationally reported high school disruptions of a serious nature during the period from November 1968 to February 1969. An overwhelming number of these protests arose from immediate student problems, including racial problems. The second most important cause of protest involved both domestic and international socio-political issues.

The seriousness of the situation is underlined by a survey conducted in the spring of 1969 by the National Association of Secondary School Principals. Three out of five high school principals reported some form of active protest in their schools. Unrest was found most extensive in the large urban and suburban schools. It is interesting to note that even among rural schools, half of the principals reported some form of unrest. It was revealed that racial questions were the most common issue in serious disruptions in the schools. The Urban Research Corporation reported that high school student protests are more racial in context than college protests. Also, the Center for the Study of Violence at Brandeis University has found that violence and overt discontent are more pervasive in high schools than in any other educational institution in the United States.

Unfortunately, the study of violence and militancy in our urban secondary schools is most timely. Concern for student involvement has been expressed by many, including Paul Putnam, associate director of the NEA's Commission on Professional Rights and Responsibilities, who said that high school protesters had employed "the tactics of boycotting classes, demonstrations, disruption of assemblies, false fire alarms and trash can fires," [1] to create tension and turmoil.

The United States Office of Education has demonstrated its interest in the problem by funding projects involving greater student participation in the decision-making processes of secondary schools.

Who are the individuals who are leading these disturbances at the secondary school level? What are their typical characteristics? What are their purposes? How do they expect to attain their goals? What specific issues have precipitated student violence? How can this violence be overcome? To obtain first-hand answers to these questions and others pertinent to the problems of militancy and violence in the urban secondary schools, the authors interviewed twelve high school students who have assumed leadership roles in recent militant actions. All came from high schools in the New York City area. That this study was conducted only in New York City and is based on interviews with only twelve militant high school

[1] *New York Times,* July 6, 1969, Section IV, p. 6.

students necessarily limits the applicability of its findings. Yet, both the difficulties encountered in the study and its findings are rich in implications for the entire nation.

How does one identify militant student leaders and then get them to speak fully to investigators? Community groups, teachers, and school administrators and students were asked to provide the authors with the names of probable student militants. Many of the young militants so identified were reluctant to share with the authors their feelings about the causes and manifestations of militancy in secondary schools. After considerable discussion, twelve students agreed to participate in this study and freely expressed their views on the contemporary high school scene.

The students interviewed were not hard-core ghetto youths. Their parents came from the ranks of the skilled, semiskilled, and professionals and generally were in sympathy with the activities of their children. Some of the black and Puerto Rican students, however, indicated that their parents had reservations concerning militant activities because they feared that their children would be penalized by the "establishment" in ways which would impede their academic success. The students said that, in general, they got along well with their parents, and their militant activities were not discussed at home.

The students indicated that the leaders in the militant movement are chosen by the student militants themselves by informal vote, the leaders usually being the most vocal and the most knowledgeable individuals. Student leaders from different schools do communicate with each other, but decisions affecting the policy of action in a particular school are made independently. When demonstrations occur at a particular school, militants from other schools are invited to participate. There is no formal committee of high school militants on a systemwide basis. Word is passed around to other schools in an informal fashion.

Religion plays a minor role in the lives of these students.

Black students, in particular, were most vocal in their contempt for religious institutions, believing that black and white churches have fed palliatives to their members in order to take their minds away from the really important problems facing the poor. In fact, the students were emphatic in their disapproval of all church-sponsored activities.

The students defined a high school militant as an individual with extremely high level of social consciousness, who is aware of the evils and injustices in society, and who feels deeply that these conditions must be corrected. He knows that he will have to make sacrifices financially, emotionally and physically to bring about these changes, and is ready to do so. This extreme social consciousness can best be illustrated by what one student militant said:

. . . live in the urban ghettos and see how black children aspire to be one thing: White! See fellow human beings who are hungry, ill-clothed, living in dilapidated housing, experiencing rampant diseases. Go out and explore. Then explore the different options that are available and then choose one. If you have this extreme social consciousness, you will devote your life to meeting the needs of all mankind.

The students viewed themselves as revolutionists: defining a revolutionist as one who is more aware and more knowledgeable of the school situation than school authorities are. They want immediate change. If the change can be achieved in a peaceful manner, that is acceptable to them. But the changes must be made, and they must come today, not tomorrow. School administrators, they point out, make changes extremely slowly, if at all, and need to be prodded. Thus, there must be marches, demonstrations, boycotts, and even violence in the cafeteria, the halls, auditorium, and the streets adjacent to the school. This violence is planned to weaken the administration's steadfastness and to bring pressures to bear by politicians and parents on the administration to consider the students' demands seriously.

The students admitted that they are a minority in their schools: a large minority and one that is rapidly growing as more students become familiar with the goals of the militants. Their attitude toward moderate students is one of disdain. The "liberal" student, according to the militants, is one who is afraid to put into deeds what he puts into words.

The black students acknowledged that there were some anti-Semitic feelings among blacks, but stressed that this is only natural. The Jews were described by these student leaders as a group that has only recently made significant social and economic progress in the United States. The militants see the Jews as the group that feels most threatened by black economic and occupational gains. The Jews occupy many civil service positions; an area in which blacks are trying to make job gains. Blacks, they say, do not hate Jews because they are Jews. Yet, these militant students are tolerant of the views of Albert Vann and Leslie Campbell, two teachers who expressed strong anti-Semitic views during the New York City teachers' strike in 1968.

Blacks who have achieved positions of prominence in public or professional life, such as Charles Wilson, former Unit Administrator of the I.S. 201 Complex, Carl Stokes, Mayor of Cleveland, and Andrew Hatcher, Mayor of Gary, Indiana, are viewed as having been successful because they appealed to black and white liberals. The students, however, now saw these men as being concerned only with furthering their own interests; they are regarded as having forgotten the black masses in the ghettos.

Throughout the course of the interviews, the students, especially the black militants, indicated that they look for leadership to such black leaders as Bobby Seale, Eldridge Cleaver, Stokeley Carmichael, and Huey Newton. Other individuals favorably mentioned are Castro, Che Guevera, and Mao. These individuals are admired by the militants because of the belief that they are concerned not only about the black community, but about all the poor. Elijah Muhammed is not especially popular among the militants interviewed. His concept of self-help and black pride is still respected, but he and the Muslims are viewed as having gone as far as they can go within the social structure. The NAACP is viewed as a failure. While recognizing that the NAACP did succeed in winning court cases and in pushing through civil rights legislation, the militants stressed that enforcement of these measures has been ineffectual. The NAACP has served a purpose in historical perspective, they admit, but now it is viewed as a hindrance in the fight for black progress.

The most popular reading material of these students are those books which focus on the life style of the blacks—such as, Michael Harrington's *The Other America*; Frantz Fanon's *White Faces, Black Masks, The Wretched of the Earth, The Dying Colonialism*; *Malcolm X Speaks, The Autobiography of Malcolm X, Red Fights Back*; Charles E. Lincoln's *The Black Muslims in America*; and the writings of Eldridge Cleaver.

Almost all of the students interviewed are planning to attend college. They intend to become lawyers, doctors, and businessmen. Yet if necessary, they will sacrifice security and all else to lead their fellow students if their pleas are ignored by the establishment.

What are the factors which contribute to precipitating secondary school disruptions? The students expressed concern over the methods by which school administrators utilize their powers to suspend students from school. The students claim that administrators use suspension as a power device to deal with students whose social, political, or racial opinions are contrary to the wishes of the establishment. The students suspect that suspension is used as a means of removing dissenting student leaders from the school situation. On the other hand, it is interesting to note, the students interviewed indicated that they will support suspensions if specific infractions are committed, provided that specific rules are established and approved by the students to whom they apply. They also believe that the power of suspension should be taken away from the principal. They suggest that students, parents, teachers, and administrators form committees to decide which rule infractions are serious enough to result in student suspensions. For example, some of the students were emphatic in their belief that student drug pushers should be suspended, as well as students who consistently physically abuse teachers and students.

They emphasized that the cause of the trouble must be determined before a suspension is made and that every means should be utilized to protect the rights of the accused. In any suspension hearing, students should be given a fair opportunity to present their side of the story with the assistance of an attorney. Under no conditions should a student be suspended for voicing an opinion in a student demonstration or for distributing written materials. There is strong feeling among the students that suspensions are related to racial problems. They believe that many black militants and their white supporters have been suspended merely for opposing white racism.

Another cause of student unrest according to the leaders interviewed is the belief that general and vocational courses offered in the high schools are archaic so far as preparation for the world of work is concerned. They point out that we are living in a time of rapid change. Society is constantly demanding specialized skills. As a result, education is more vital to individual success than it was in previous years. General and vocational diplomas mean nothing in the contemporary occupational market. As one vocational school graduate said, "It's like you just sat there and didn't do anything. I wasn't trained to do anything when I graduated!"

The belief is prevalent that in order to overcome the antiquated terminal type of education, our schools must recruit more, and better, guidance counselors with an understanding of minority group problems. More effective teachers are needed so that a greater percentage of environmentally handicapped youth will be able to attend two-year or four-year colleges upon graduation. Special tutorial help in the pre–high school grades is needed to prepare students from disadvantaged circumstances. If necessary, these special tutoring programs must be continued in the high school. In essence, these students are seeking quality teaching, an updated curriculum, tutorial assistance, and teacher sensitivity.

The students also expressed the thought that the high school program need not be completed in three or four years. The student should carry the number of academic subjects which would not cause him to be overwhelmed by homework or leave him insufficient time to deal with the more complex or sequential subjects. The most important consideration should be the student's successful completion of his academic work, not the number of years he needs to do this.

The students also opposed compulsory attendance laws as they are now constituted, and expressed the thought that students who want to learn will go to school, provided that the school has something to offer. If a student does not want to learn, either he will not come to school, or he will merely go through the motions of coming to school, or become a discipline problem. Rather than enforce compulsory attendance, they suggested a compulsory, relevant curriculum designed to meet the needs and interest of today's students. To ensure a relevant curriculum, they said the students must be contributing partners. If a school is in a predominantly black area, greater emphasis should be placed on the role of the black society. White or black, the students must be able to relate to the curriculum which is offered.

The students demanded the implementation of black studies programs. Since black contributions to the development of the United States have been overlooked in the past, there is a feeling among the militants that his condition can be rectified only through a separate black studies program. All the students interviewed see the "return to Africa" movements as unrealistic at this time; however, an understanding of the developments in black Africa was one of their primary concerns.

Most of the students described the general atmosphere in their schools as dangerously tense. They commented that there is friction between black and white students. The sudden surge of black pride and militancy, coupled with the black students' desire for social change, has surprised many white students and created a further gap between the races. The white students frequently reflect the attitude of their parents toward blacks and behave accordingly. The black students retaliate in order to save face and to maintain a balance of power. The outcome is conflict, and too often armed combat is the end result.

The students pointed out that, in general, they have lost respect for their teachers. They feel teachers have put selfish interests before the legitimate welfare of their students. There is no doubt that participation in teacher strikes has created distrust among the students and has aggravated the racial conflict in the schools. The students insisted, however, that they judge teachers on an individual basis; no blanket indictment is intended. Some teachers who participated in the New York City teachers' strike in 1968 are still respected because they have rapport with their students and are effective teachers. On the other hand, some teachers who came to school when the strikes were occurring are still regarded as untrustworthy and poor teachers.

Effective teachers, according to the students, are those who show concern for students and who are sound instructional taskmasters. The young militants have little appreciation, if any, for the profession's regard for graduate degrees. The students look only to performance and sense when a teacher goes "all out for them."

Tenure laws, it was emphasized, perpetuate the life of ineffective teachers and by their cumbersome machinery prevent interested parents from exerting pressure to remove ineffective teachers from the classrooms. The students emphasize that skin color does not determine a teacher's ability. Black teachers can be just as effective or ineffective as white teachers.

The students acknowledged that violence should be utilized only as a last alternative. Only if all other means fail to achieve a particular goal should violence be considered. However, if violence is the only device that brings change, then it must be used. Burning of buildings, disruption of class, demonstrations, and physical assaults on teachers must be utilized to bring about success. The students did not hesitate to point out that violence on college campuses has indeed brought about some changes which would not likely have come about if left to the college administrators or trustees.

The militants wholeheartedly support disruptions on college campuses. However, they pointed out that the high school and college movements are not a unified front. According to the students interviewed, the disruptions in the high schools are not being organized by college students. The college and high school movements are two distinct operations with many common goals. It was emphasized that only high school students determine the policies for high school student action.

According to the students interviewed, high school militancy is actually an extension of an overall movement taking place today in the United States. Students in America today are beginning to realize that what happened in the streets of Los Angeles, Chicago, and Newark is now occurring in the high schools. Changes have to be made. It would be unrealistic, however, to expect these changes to take place without violence because of the very fabric of our society. As one student said:

People respect fear. They respect force. You can go out and petition all day and all night, but if you don't actually draw blood or take some definite action, you will be ignored. People down through the years have respected fear. You have to show that you are capable of taking actions which will promote fear and endanger them and their family.

Regarding the racial situation in the country, the students unanimously stated that if the power structure is willing to accept the necessary social changes, then violence will not pit black against white. The establishment, according to the students, consists of the political power structure on the local, state, and federal levels. Those who control the money and, thus, the power are part of this establishment.

The students agreed that blacks in America are too small a minority to work alone. As a result, blacks must form alliances with white groups that believe in the black cause. The students believed that the community also should have a voice in deciding what children are taught. The militants strongly believe that students and community organizations can work together to improve the urban schools. Community and neighborhood control of local schools permeated the discussions.

The students expressed with firmness their conviction that the major objective of the high school militant movement is to give students an equal voice in the activities and policies of the school. School policy should originate with the students and should be decisive. The students frequently expressed the sentiment that if you are not organized and do not exert pressure on the administration, you cannot have student power.

The black students were emphatic in their conviction that drug traffic in the schools should be eliminated completely. They stated that this can be done by having students learn who the pushers are, and then driving them out of the school. Police and teachers alone cannot do this successfully. The white students interviewed expressed the view that the drug pushers should not be driven out of the school. They felt that students should retain the option of deciding whether or not to purchase drugs. This was one of the few areas in which the black and white students differed.

While many school administrators and teachers may dismiss the views of these militants whom we have interviewed as the opinions of only a handful of the school population, to do so is a serious mistake. Even though these students are indeed in the minority, there is substantial feeling among students of all political and social persuasion that changes must be made in the decision-making processes within the high schools. The school establishment must make some changes, not only for the purpose of avoiding student confrontations, but to initiate sound educational policy. Significant changes can and must be implemented.

Today's students are tomorrow's political, economic and social leaders. In a democratic system which depends so much on the choices made by its constituents, intelligent participation in the democratic processes is an essential part of education. Involvement in school affairs at the decision-making level offers students meaningful social relations with peers and adults and exposes them to a variety of ideas and points of view. Up to now, colleges and secondary schools have dealt with student demands for a voice in shaping their own destinies in a multiplicity of ways, most of which have not been acceptable to students.

We can no longer afford to wait for the Students for a Democratic Society (SDS) to provide the stimulus for change in the schools. It is long overdue that educational leaders implement social policies before the picketers arrive at their gates. We cannot ignore student concerns regarding dress, hair length, smoking, racial relations, sex education, censorship of students, effective teaching, relevant curriculum, and a host of other issues.

Now is the time for our schools to initiate communication, rather than after the riot. True, recent student riots and unrest have caused considerable consternation in adult circles. Students in our high schools, however, like students in our universities and colleges, are beginning to resent the perennial parental role of our secondary schools. Unrest frequently develops into threats only after the school administrators have refused to meet with the student leaders to discuss critical issues.

If responsible educators fail to act on the legitimate requests of the sensible majority of their students, not only will they be playing directly into the hands of the minority of professional revolutionists, who thrive on establishment stubborness and myopia, but they will be perpetuating a system of education that is failing. The longer it takes for real, constructive changes to take place in schools, the greater the possibility that schools will become battlegrounds. Battlegrounds—"establishment" versus "youth"—with all the implements of destruction: guns, knives and bombs. Now is the time to act!

11

The Unanswered Questions

HARRY N. RIVLIN

When I was invited to write the last chapter, I chose "The Unanswered Questions" as my topic because I was certain that, as this book concludes, there would be many unanswered questions. In fact, the better the book, the greater the number of unanswered questions there should be.

In my discussions with teachers of ghetto children, two questions are asked repeatedly: "Now that I have been made to feel guilty, what do I do?" Another type of question comes from those who are community oriented rather than school oriented. Their question is, "What do you do with teachers who are arrogant, who seem to be saying, 'We lifted ourselves up by our bootstraps, why don't they?' and do not realize we have no bootstraps with which to pull ourselves up."

Each of these groups has other questions to which it wants immediate answers. Yet, there are no immediate answers, no short cuts and no miracle drugs. In fact, much of our difficulty today arises from short cuts we have taken in the past. Miracle drugs are just not available for such complex problems. After observing an Urban League Street Academy in action, I was impressed. I thought, "Here is the answer." Then, as I reflected on this hope, I came to realize that there is no *the* answer.

One of the depressing conclusions to be drawn from the history of education is that it can be summarized as a sequence of formalism, a reaction against formalism, and then the reaction becoming as formal as the formalism it had replaced. One of the problems of the tremendous range of educational innovations now being implemented in the country is that the innovation is successful only as long as the people who started the innovation conduct it. Once it is adopted as a standard course of study or a uniform type of school organization, it loses something.

The American people are fairly well dressed, and they dress so well, not because of the custom tailors and dressmakers who design clothing for the select few, but because of the needle trades factories on Seventh Avenue in New York City that manufacture clothing wholesale. One of the unanswered questions in education is how we can take a promising development and adopt it as standard operating procedure. How can we take a custom made program and run it wholesale? The cloak and suit industry can do it with clothing. Why can't we do it in education?

I think we shall never find miracle drugs to cure our educational ills until we employ people who can administer them effectively. Fortunately, such people are all around us—we should appreciate their ability and capitalize on their potential. We are living in an age of technology, and in a technological world it is easy to forget that the individual is still the key person.

In that fantastic flight to the moon, our astronauts profited from the most advanced technology we had developed. Both on earth and in space, there were highly sophisticated computers. Yet, when the lunar module approached the surface of the moon, the computers cried, "Alarm" and it was then that the astronauts took control and manually completed the descent. In the last analysis, the computers gave up and the individuals took over.

The individual is as important today as he was when Immanuel Kant uttered his famous dictum, "So live as to treat every human being as an end in himself, not as a means to an end." What would happen if every teacher treated every child as an end in himself and not as a means to an end? What would happen if every principal treated every teacher as an end in himself? At the very least, this would be a more wholesome world in which to live.

On a recent trip to the Educational Testing Service at Princeton, I was taken "behind the counter" where I saw two fabulous machines. They have a computer which has reels that can record 20,000 to 50,000 separate test items and, in addition, note 10 characteristics for each item, such as, grade level, index of difficulty, and subject matter. The committee of which I was part was invited to order a test constructed according to our specifications. Like all other wise guys, we wanted to trick the computer and so we requested as complicated a test as we could conceive. Thus, we wanted a test of 50 items which had w number of items that 90 percent of fifth graders could answer correctly and x number of items that only 10 percent of high school seniors could answer correctly; we wanted y number of items from literature and z number from science. It really was a tricky test.

The computer went to work and wheels started spinning forward and in reverse as in a Rube Goldberg contraption. After some test items had been tentatively selected, they had to be rejected and others substituted because of the specificity of our instructions. For example, the science question it accepted might change the total number of questions that 90 percent of the fifth graders could answer correctly. We left the computer with its wheels spinning and moved to another one.

Any teacher who has ever had to grade hundreds of true-false or multiple choice items will appreciate the second computer that can grade both sides of the paper at once, read the pupil's name, and then print the name and the score at the rate of 233 per minute. If you were just going to flip the pages, you could not do it as rapidly as this machine prints the name and the score.

By the time we had looked at these computers some thirty minutes had elapsed and we returned to the room in which we were meeting. Waiting for us was the test we had ordered, selected and printed according to our specifications.

It was an amazing performance until we realized that how good the test was did not depend upon the machine at all, but rather upon the wisdom and the knowledge of the persons who wrote the test items. How valid the score was that they got at the rate of 233 a minute depended upon how valid the items were to begin with. If the items were ridiculous or irrelevant, we got a ridiculous or irrelevant score in a fraction of the time that would otherwise be necessary. It must be remembered that consensus of useless opinion is a useless consensus of opinion. Despite all of our technological advance, I must return to the role of the individual: the individual teacher, principal, child, and parent, for it is these people who make education succeed or fail.

When Knute Rocke was at the height of his coaching career at Notre Dame, he was asked by a friend why he let scouts from other colleges watch his team at practice. Wasn't he afraid they would steal his plays? His answer was, "It isn't the play that wins the game. It's the execution." When you think of imaginative plans conceived by imaginative superintendents, we must never forget that whether the plans are successful depends upon the execution, upon the concern and competence of the teachers and administrators who will translate the plan into reality.

We are in a period of rapid educational change, whether we

like it or not. We have seen more changes in education in the last ten years than in the previous fifty, and the changes we have seen are as nothing compared with the changes that are about to occur throughout America. It is only natural that people should react emotionally to changes that involve them personally. Demands for change, moreover, usually come not as rational requests but as highly emotional demands. It was Bernard Shaw who said that inventors are usually unreasonable people because reasonable people see no need for change.

When the demands for change are emotional, we cannot afford to react with equal emotion. We have three possible procedures to follow. First, we can ignore the demands, but this is impossible today. The second reaction is for us to become defensive and explain why the change is not needed. This, too, is not feasible today. There is, however, a third procedure. I think that what we have to do is look at the demands for change, however reasonable or unreasonable the demand may be, try to see exactly what the critic wants, and then see how to satisfy his demand.

Considering the changes that are occurring and the likelihood of even more changes, I do not want to give the impression that American education is bankrupt. The United States has achieved something in education that is unprecedented. The United States is the only nation that has changed higher education from a privileged institution for the intellectually or socially elite and made it practically a part of the common school system. Fred Hechinger, in Chapter 1, referred to the educational successes of Scandinavia, which is certainly in the forefront of social progress in some areas. Yet, the percentage of American youth going to college is much greater than the percentage of Scandinavian youth attending the universities.

In 1842 the citizens of New York organized a Board of Education, and only five years later, in 1847, New Yorkers by popular vote organized the Free Academy—which has since grown into the great City University of New York. The date is significant. This was 1847, at a time when not even the most advanced countries of the world had universal elementary and secondary education, but New Yorkers established a free college.

Dr. Robert Havighurst, when he came to Fordham University as its first John Mosler Professor of Urban Education, listed some six ways in which education today is far ahead of where it was thirty, forty, or fifty years ago. He said, "First, we have better textbooks and better curriculum; second, our schools are better equipped with libraries, laboratories and other special rooms; third, our schools are staffed by teachers with more years of education than they had earlier; fourth, we have smaller classes; fifth, there are more special classes for children with various types of abilities; and sixth, schools are doing a better job of freeing children and youth to learn on their own."

In short, education in America is pretty good—and that is the trouble. Pretty good just is not good enough in times of enormous potential and tremendous problems. As a graduate student (my field was educational psychology), I had the privilege of studying with E. L. Thorndike. We were sure then that once we knew how children learn, we would know how to teach them. We were equally as sure that we had discovered how children learn. There were all kinds of brilliant experiments to demonstrate how learning took place. In one of them, a cat, who had been properly prepared for the experiment by going without food, learned how to push a ball into a depression in the floor so that the trap door opened and he could get the piece of fish he wanted. The cat even learned later how to pull a string to release the ball that he then pushed into the depression in order to get his food.

We drew innumerable conclusions from such experiments as these. The cat learned because he was ready to learn. He could perform what he was asked to perform. He knew when he was successful, and he was rewarded every time he succeeded.

There were more implications, too. We were sure that education could now become a science, because we could demonstrate scientifically how learning took place.

The difficulty, of course, is that while learning is a cognitive process, it is also a social process. Every classroom in the country is crowded, no matter what the size of the class register, because when a child comes to school, he does not come alone. He brings his family, his friends, and his whole cultural background. To teach as though all that matters is his intellectual processes is to ignore a basic component. Educators must ask, "How do you teach a black high school student once he realizes that a white dropout earns more than a black high school graduate?" "How do you teach a youngster who comes to school knowing that everybody knows he just cannot learn?" His teachers know it and do not even expect him to learn. Even his grandmother knows it. The last thing she said when he was leaving home that morning was, "You are exactly like your father, and he was no good, either." How can we teach if we ignore the crucial matter of the youngster's background, his hopes and fears, wishes and frustrations?

I think we can begin by concentrating on teaching rather than on explaining why children do not learn. Joseph Monserrat has urged that Spanish speaking children must not be thought inferior because they have difficulty with the English language. We must ignore the various labels that have been used to describe the children who are not learning what we want to teach. When you go to a dentist because you have a toothache, the one thing you want from him is that he stop the toothache. If the dentist were to draw a picture of your jaw and explain why, with a jaw like that, it is only natural that you should have a toothache, your reaction would be a simple one: "Stop the toothache!"

As professionals, teachers should apply themselves to their job instead of speaking of how hard they work and how late they stayed up last night preparing a lesson plan that turned out to be ineffective. Teachers should assume that students can learn provided that it is worth their while to learn; that teachers let them learn; and that teachers get help in discovering ever more effective ways of teaching them.

When I say "making it worth their while to learn," I think of the first question any teacher ought to ask when he starts to prepare a lesson for any group. If this were a lesson on the Industrial Revolution, the first question is not "What was the Industrial Revolution?" or "Why was it important?" The first question should be: "If I were fifteen years old, and I lived on the corner of Lincoln Avenue and Main Street, what would I want to know about the Industrial Revolution?" If teachers begin their planning with the point of contact, it is more likely to touch the individual child, than if they begin with the topic and teach the Industrial Revolution as they would teach it on Houston Street on New York City's East Side or in Houston, Texas.

When I say, "let them learn," I am thinking of the Pilgrim's Monument in Provincetown, Massachusetts, which is the easiest monument in the world to climb. It is a copy of a French monument which was built by Napoleon, who wanted a monument he could climb on horseback. The climb begins with a ramp, a step just a few inches high—any youngster can step that high. Then there is a ramp leading to the far corner. It is a gradual incline. Anybody can walk it. At that corner, there is another step of a few inches and another ramp. At each corner a step and a ramp, step and ramp, and you are at the top before you realize you have climbed.

That is what the teaching machine tries to do, and a teacher is the most sophisticated teaching machine that has ever been designed. There have been many mathematics teachers who, because they know their material, go through the problem they are solving at the blackboard very quickly, skipping steps, then brushing the chalk dust off their hands ask, "Are there any questions?" There are no questions because the students did not understand anything. The same math can be taught successfully if it is taught in smaller steps. How short the steps should be and how steep the ramps should be will vary from person to person, and from subject to subject. Basically, anything can be taught if we make it worth the youngster's while to learn it and if we present it in ways that he can learn.

The student's difficulty in learning is sometimes a result of the teacher's ineptness in presenting the material. Teaching is difficult; teaching is a miracle. That a teacher, by controlling the flow of air over his vocal chords, should change how people act, how people think, how people feel is really a miracle. Educators must not be overwhelmed by a sense of failure if they do not perform miracles every hour for every person. But the question, "How can we be more effective in our teaching?" still remains, or, better, "How can children be more effective in their learning?"

Here our pupils can become the teachers. The adage is true that we learn much from our teachers, more from our colleagues, and most from our pupils. Unlike supervisors who may visit a classroom only occasionally, the pupil is there all the time and the pupil is often a better judge of what is happening to him in the classroom than anyone else. A procedure that I have found to be extremely helpful in my own teaching career is to involve the students in an evaluation of my course. Near the end of the term, I ask my students to answer three questions about the course or the class, not about me as a teacher.

1. Since this course is to be taught again next term, which features of this course, as you had it, would you keep?

2. What would you change?

3. Are there any other comments about this course that you want to make?

In order to avoid embarrassment and to encourage frankness, students are asked not to sign their comments.

Putting the questions in terms of the course rather than the teacher makes it seem less like a bid for verbal bouquets. For me, these comments have been invaluable. There has not been a class that did not respond to the questions with all the seriousness I could have wished. There has not been a term in which I have not found suggestions I could employ the succeeding term. Asking students to indicate the features they wanted retained was as helpful as asking them to indicate the changes they thought should be introduced, for it enabled me to evaluate how widely a specific change was wanted. One reassuring aspect of these comments is that students never tried merely to make the course easier or pleasanter. They did not mind working hard, provided that they saw that the work was important for achieving a goal they recognized as worth reaching.

It is unfair to demand that students be specific and constructive in their comments. If the students say that they find their textbook too difficult to understand, we should not expect them to be able to analyze the author's style in order to indicate how it can be made clearer to adolescents. Nor should we expect them to be so familiar with the literature in a subject that they can suggest a better textbook for us to use. They are being helpful enough if they get us to look for a more appropriate book or to find better means of teaching them how to use the book that is prescribed by the school authorities.

I have found students' written comments to be an excellent means of supplementing the oral comments made in class or in conversation. Most students are too easily embarrassed to tell you directly anything that is too damning or too flattering. When a student does say something to us, we have no way of knowing whether he is reflecting only his personal point of view or one that is widely held. It is well worth the few minutes it takes to get the reactions of all the students.

I am sure that we will respect the opinions expressed by students, otherwise we would not ask for them, but we must not attach so much importance to them that we accept every suggestion uncritically. Some of their criticisms may be petty, and others may relieve minor problems only to create more serious ones. It is better to treat their suggestions as raising questions you should consider, not as commands to be obeyed unhesitatingly. But as Sheldon Marcus and Philip Vairo pointed out in the preceeding chapter, "Now is the time for our schools to initiate communication. . . . If responsible educators fail to respond to the legitimate requests of the sensible majority of their students, not only will they be playing directly into the hands of the minority of professional revolutionists who thrive on establishment stubborness and myopia, but they will be perpetuating a system of education that is failing."

One of the major changes that has taken place in education is in the relationship between the school and the community. Traditionally, it was the school that took the initiative in educational planning. Then, to establish good community relations, the school went to the community and explained what the school was trying to do. Those schools thought they had a good school-community program and tried to use the resources of the community (material and human) in implementing the school's program. School administrators thought they were being most gracious when they let the community use the auditorium when they had no other use for it. This is no longer enough. In Chapter 6 Elliott Shapiro has written eloquently about the parents who came to school, were treated shabbily, and never returned. Why should parents return to a place where they are abused?

There has been almost a complete change in the relationship between the school and the community it services. In some communities, the level of education of the residents is as high, if not higher, than that of the school staff. These people now ask, "Why should the teachers and principals be the only ones to decide what the school is to do?" In other communities, there is the feeling (remember, whether it is justified or not does not matter) that the school just has not been meeting their needs. The community, therefore, wants a voice in making the educational plans. It is the community that now rightly asks, "How do we tell the school what we would like to do, and how can we use the school resources in implementing the plan that the community has developed?

Reverend Oliver has said that the community wants more than a voice in school affairs: it wants control. He says that "community control is nothing more than local self-government, the urgency and necessity of which is deeply felt in communities throughout the country." (See p. 122). Educators are then confronted with another problem. If you have two people from the community in the principal's office, both of whom claim to speak for and represent *the* community, the principal must play detective. Thus, it is important for administrators to know beforehand who really represents the community. Educators must try to respond to the legitimate requests of community representatives, always remembering not to be intimidated by those who make the most noise.

I was personally involved at Fordham with just this kind of problem, about three years ago. Fordham was one of sixty places in the country asked to develop a program for training the teacher trainers. The rationale for the TTT program is that if you are trying to change education, you have to influence teachers, but it is difficult to reach two million teachers. If you could influence the people who train the teachers, you could get change more quickly.

Fordham began by assembling a group of about fifteen from the college of liberal arts, school of education and the New York City school system. A week later, we came up with a program. We then invited members of the community to meet with us to see how we could implement it. We were working with the school district in which TTT is now located, and so we went to the three community groups in this area: Central Harlem Community Corporation (HARYOU-ACT, Inc.); Mid-West Side Community Planning Committee; Lower West Side Community Corporation. I presented our plan to this meeting.

Mayor La Guardia used to say that he made very few boners, but when he did, each one was a beaut. One of my prize boners was when I presented the plan which people from Fordham and other schools had evolved. The reaction on the part of the community group could be summarized in one question, "And who asked you to?" We were taken aback when we realized that the community is no longer willing to play the part of the grateful recipient of favors that are handed out from above. What we did was to scrap the plan and began anew.

What we have now is a plan that was developed cooperatively by these community representatives, school people, and faculty members working on a parity basis. The Policy Committee, which is the governing body for the whole program, consists of fourteen voting members and four nonvoting members. The fourteen voting members include six people from the community, elected by the community organizations; four from the school system, with two administrators chosen by the assistant superintendent and two teachers chosen by the faculty of the two schools in which we were working; four from Fordham University, two from liberal arts and two from the school of education—in each case, one is a student and the other is a faculty member. In short, we have one member of the school of education on the Policy Committee of fourteen. There are four nonvoting members. One is the director of the project; the second is the chairman of the school board; the third is the assistant superintendent of the district; the fourth is the dean of the school of education. I come to the meetings not with the voice of authority—I do not even have a vote—but with the authority of my voice. If I had to choose between the two, I would rather have the authority of voice.

Each member of the Policy Committee has a vote that is equal to anyone else's, regardless of whether he came from the schools, the community, or the college, and all receive the same honorarium. The only person who does not get an honorarium is the dean, who cannot accept an honorarium for anything that is done within his jurisdiction.

We have selected a number of participants for various TTT activities. We have, for example, a Career Ladder Program for paraprofessionals. These paraprofessionals were selected by the community and then Fordham examined their credentials to see whether they met our standards for admission. The results of this TTT activity has been a marked change in the relationship between the schools, the community, and Fordham. It was TTT that helped Fordham start a program of urban studies.

When one thinks of New York and other urban areas, one usually thinks of their problems. They also have assets. These days, when we see the word *urban*, we know that immediately following it will come either *problem* or *crisis*. How many people come to New York from a distant place because they want to see our smog at firsthand? How many come here because they want to see what crowded subways or nonoperating trains look like? People come to New York because of its theaters, its museums, its businesses, its restaurants, and its other attractions.

I am going to turn to the theater for my next theme. The theme I am going to take is not "Promises, Promises," because of those we have had enough. Instead, I go to "Man of La Mancha" and to one part of it, where Don Quixote says, "Think not of what thou art, but of what thou canst become." I think that is how we should approach our youngsters.

Chancellors, superintendents, and assistant superintendents have tremendous influence on the lives of the children, but how much children learn is affected much more directly by the individual teachers, individual principals, the individual guidance workers.

We are entering a new era of education. We have tremendous public interest, and we can accomplish more with interest than we can with apathy. We have more money than we ever thought we would get for education. It is not enough, but one of the fallacies of education is that there are no problems in education that money will not solve. I think this is a fallacy because, when we have ideas but no money to implement them, we are frustrated; but when we have money with no ideas, then we have absolute waste. At any rate, we have more money and have more gadgets. Whether audio-visual equipment improves our teaching does not depend upon whether it cost $40,000 or $80,000. It depends upon how the material is put to use.

I come back, therefore, to my original theme. It is the individual who counts. Messrs. Shanker, Marcus, Vairo, Dentler, Kvaraceus, and the other contributors to this book have outlined the revolutionary changes in American education that are opening a new era in American education. Many people, however, pronounce *era* as though it were *error*. Is it a new era or just one more error? Whether we are headed for a new era or a new error depends upon the teachers, the principals, the guidance workers, the people in the community. In the final analysis, they will tell us how to pronounce the word.

Index

academic diploma, 23–24, 149
academic results, of compensatory education, 25–27
Addams, Jane, 20
adult education, 91, 92
Afro-American studies, 14, 17
Afro-American Teachers' Association, 104–105
Alger, Horatio, 98
alienation, of schools, 34–36
Allen, James E., 120
American Civil Liberties Union, 121
American Federation of Labor and Congress of Industrial Organizations (AFL-CIO), 134
American Federation of Teachers, 47; urban representation, 143
American Medical Association, 16
Antioch College, 77
anti-Semitism, 164
Aristotle, 111, 112
authority structure, 47
Autobiography of Malcolm X, 165

Baltimore, 143
Banneker Project, St., Louis, 26–27
Belkin, Natalie, 118
Bellevue Hospital, Psychiatric Division, 97
bilingual instruction, 74, 126–127
Black Muslims in America, 165
black power, 47, 118
black studies, 32, 167–168
black teachers, 104–105, 127
Bloomfield, Jack, 118
Board of Education, N.Y.C., 38, 107, 109, 128, 137; decentralization, 116, 127; Ocean Hill-Brownsville district, 115, 116, 119, 120
Boris Gudunov, 113
Bortner, Doyle, 79–94
Boston, 143
Brandeis University, Center for the Study of Violence, 161
bridge generation, Puerto Rican, 155, 158

Bronx Community College, 24
Brooklyn College, 24
Brown, Claude, 48, 49, 57
Burden of Blame, 121

Campbell, Leslie, 164
Career Ladder Program, 186
career plans, 165
Carmichael, Stokeley, 164
Castro, Fidel, 165
CBS Radio, 121
Center for Urban Education, 65, 66, 67, 70
Central Harlem Community Corporation, 185
certification, 98
Cervantes, Lucius F., 43
Chicago, 9, 133, 143, 146, 169
child guidance centers, 53
C.H.I.L.D. Project, 70
Chinese, principal, in N.Y.C., 131
church, and education, 115
City College, New York, 24
Civil Rights Acts, 16
civil rights groups, 148
civil rights, teacher's, 133, 142–143
City University, New York, 177
Clark, Kenneth, 30
Clark, Mayme, 30
class size, 10, 144
Cleaver, Eldridge, 164, 165
Cleveland, 143
clique-group structure, in schools, 49–50
Cloward, Richard, 42
Coleman Report, 146
College Careers, 75–76
colleges: campus violence, 160, 169; minority enrollment, 24; Negro, 5; open admission, 4; private, 6–7
Columbia University, Center for Research and Education on American Liberties, 160
commercial diploma, 149
Commission on Civil Rights, 27
community agencies, and schools, 63
community control, 5, 38–39, 47, 170; bilingual instruction, 126–127; church, state, and home, 115; decentralization, 116; and

democracy, 112, 113–114; defined, 111; and parental approval, 125; parents and teachers, 128–129, 130; vs. power structure, 114; professional accountability, 123; quality of education, 123, 128; right of self-government, 112–113, 122; school taxes, 130–131; segregation, 123–124; teacher rights, 129–130; teacher strike, N.Y.C., 1967, 118; vs. teacher unions, 116, 125; *see also* Ocean Hill-Brownsville
compensatory alternatives, for poor instruction, 71–73, 74, 75
compensatory education, 7, 19–20; academic results of, 25–27; academic vs. general diplomas, 23–24; alienation of school, 34–36; college enrollment, among minorities, 24; cultural deprivation hypothesis, 19, 25, 28–30, 31–32; curricula materials, 32–34; dropout rate, 20–21, 23, 26; failures of, 27–36, 66; history of, 20–21; home visitation, 35–36; vs. integration, 21–22, 27; learning ability, of culturally deprived, 30–31; noneducation, 22–25; parental interest, 35–36; professional responsibility, 36–39; reading retardation, 22–23, 31; socially disadvantaged hypothesis, 19, 25, 28–30, 31–32
compulsory attendance, 167
Conant, James B., 16, 52
Congress, U.S., 110
conservatism, in education, 16, 18
Cornell University, 109
cultural deprivation, hypothesis of, 19, 25, 28–30, 31–32
cultural renewal, and the schools, 56–58
curricula, overt vs. covert, 58–59

decentralization, 88, 116, 127
decision-making, and students, 171–172
delinquency, 50–54, 63; correlation with dropping-out, 41–42; extent

of, 40–41; group profile, 42–45; prediction of, 59–62; and reading retardation, 59–60; and school work structure, 46–47
Delinquency and Opportunity, 42
democracy: American, 114; and education, 85–86, 101, 102, 112, 113–114; Greek, 112, 114; participatory, 114; Western, 113–114
demonstration districts, origin of, 127
Demonstration Guidance Project, New York, 25
Dentler, Robert A., 64–68, 187
Detroit, 143
diploma: academic, 23–24, 149; commercial, 149; general, 23–24, 149, 166; vocational, 166
disadvantaged, defined, 67–68
Disadvantaged, The: Challenge to Education, 34
disruptive child, 104
District 3, N.Y.C., 109
Donovan, Bernard, 119, 126, 128
draft, military, 15–16
dropout rates, 20–21, 23, 26, 41–42, 56, 65, 66–67, 97–98, 149
dropouts, percentage of, 40–41
drugs, 15, 170–171
Dying Colonialism, 165

education, 6–7; class size, 10; conservatism, 16, 18; decentralization, 88, 116, 127; drugs, 15; elitist, 85–86; as existentialist togetherness, 6; federal aid, 109–110; internships, 16; kibbutz, 75; minority group teachers, 17, 104–105, 131; preschool centers, U.S., 10; professionalism, 13, 15, 16, 46, 133, 179–180; pupil evaluation of teaching, 181–183; quality of, 123, 128, 181; research on, 7; street academies, 6; teacher aides, 10–11, 16; teacher ineptness, 181; teacher training, 16–17; teacher unions, 10, 13; teaching aids, 17–18; television, 18; universal national service, 15–16; upgrading

of minorities, 17; young teachers, 13–16; *see also* schools
education, of disadvantaged: bilingual language instruction, 74; C.H.I.L.D. Project, 70; College Careers program, 75–76; community participation, 75; compensatory alternatives for poor instruction, 71–73, 74, 75; disadvantaged defined, 67–68; dropout rate, 66–67; fun and games, 75–76; IPI program, 73–74, 75; isolation of minorities, 64, 65; Language Acquisition Project, 70–71; mastery of skills, 68–70; poverty, 64–65, 66; social education program, 74; welfare dependency, 65–66
Educational Testing Service, 175
elitist education, 85–86
English language, and Puerto Ricans, 152–153, 179
Epstein, Jay, 121
ERIC, 67
ethnic warfare, 5
Exceptional Children, 59
existentialist togetherness, and education, 6

Fanon, Frantz, 165
Fantini, Mario, 34
fascism, 6
Feldman, Sandy, 118
Feretti, Fred, 121
first generation, Puerto Rican, 154–155, 158
Ford Foundation, 11, 25, 116
Fordham University, TTT program, 184–186
four-year course, and high school militancy, 167
Fox Land High School, 140
Free Academy, N.Y.C., 177, 178
Fuentes, Louis, 126
fun and games, educational, 75–76
Fund for the Advancement of Education, 11
Futurama, 3–4

Galamison, Milton, 75
generation gap, 50–51

Goodman, Paul, 75–76
Governor's Commission on the Los Angeles riots, 66
Graves, W. A., 55
Great Cities School Improvement Program, 25, 27
Great Neck, Long Island, 127–128
grievance procedures, 137–138, 143
group intelligence tests, 99–100, 101
Guevera, Ernesto (Che), 165

Harlem Preparatory School, 6, 31
Harrington, Michael, 165
HARYOU-ACT, Inc., 185
Hatcher, Andrew, 164
Havighurst, Robert, 178
Headstart (*see* Project Headstart)
Hechinger, Fred M., 3–18, 177
Higher Horizons Program, 25, 26, 71
high school militancy: administrative power of suspension, 165–166; anti-Semitism, 164; black studies, 167–168; black-white conflict, 168; career plans, 165; and college campus violence, 160, 169; community control, 170; vs. compulsory attendance, 167; defined, 163; drug traffic, 170–171; vs. four-year course, 167; general diplomas, 166; incidence, 160–161; leadership, 162, 164–165; vs. Negro establishment, 165; racial issues, 161, 170; religion, 162–163; student power, 170; students, and decision-making, 171–172; teacher competence, 168–169; teacher tenure laws, 169; violence, 169; vocational diplomas, 166
Holmes, Oliver Wendell, 83
home visitation by teachers, 35–36, 93
Hunter College, 24

immigrants, Puerto Rican, 150–152, 157–158
Income and Welfare in the United States, 65
Indians, 20
Individual Prescribed Instructional

(IPI) System of Research for Better Schools, Incorporated, 73–74
integration, 131–132; vs. compensatory education, 21–22, 27
intelligence quotient (IQ), 67, 99, 100
intelligence, and reading achievement, 99, 100
internships, teaching, 16
Israel, 75; kibbutz education, 8

Jencks, Christopher, 146
Jewish dropout rate, 98
Johnson, Herbert, 124
Junior High School Summer Program, N.Y.C., 71
Junior High School 43, N.Y.C., 25; JHS 201, 127; JHS 271, 14–15, 118, 122, 124, 129

Kant, Immanuel, 175
Kempton, Murray, 121
kibbutz education, 75
Kvaraceus, William C., 40–63, 187

labor unions, 148
Language Acquisition Project, 70–71
leadership, of high school militants, 162, 164–165
learning ability, of culturally deprived, 30–31
Leningrad, 9
Lincoln, Abraham, 81
Lincoln, Charles E., 165
Locke, John, 113
Long Island, 145
Los Angeles, 169
Lower West Side Community Corporation, 185

McCoy, Rhody, 116, 117, 119, 126
Malcolm X Speaks, 165
Manchild in the Promised Land, 48, 49
Manhattan Community College, 24
Mao Tse-tung, 165
Marcus, Sheldon, 160–172, 183, 187
Mexican-Americans, 17, 20
Mexican War, 153

middle class, 4, 10; values, 5
Mid-West Side Community Planning Committee, 185
Milwaukee, 143
minorities, 4, 17, 64, 65
Mohammed, Elijah, 165
Monserrat, Joseph, 149–159, 179
Montesquieu, C. L. de S., 113
More Effective Schools Program, 27, 73
Morgan, James, 65
Moscow, 9
Mt. Kisco, New York, 140
Moynihan, Daniel P., 64, 65
Muslims, 165

National Advisory Council on the Education of Disadvantaged Children, 54
National Association for the Advancement of Colored People (NAACP), 165
National Association of Intergroup Relations Officials, 21–22
National Association of Secondary School Principals, 160
National Education Association (NEA), 47, 52, 55, 134; Commission on Professional Rights and Responsibilities, 161; desegregation issue, 16; as rural organization, 143
nationalism, 131
National Teacher Corps, 13
needle trades, N.Y.C., 174
Negroes, 17, 20, 38, 49, 58, 102–103, 104, 118, 122, 148, 154, 162, 167; academic vs. general diplomas, 23–24; black establishment, 165; college enrollment, 24; colleges, 5; dropouts, 23; reading retardation, 22–23; school integration, 21, 22, 27; taxes, 130–131
Newark, 169
New Mexico, as bilingual state, 153
news media, and Ocean Hill-Brownsville, 121, 126
Newton, Huey, 164
New York City, 9, 20, 26, 27, 31, 35, 38, 67, 74, 107, 110, 142,
180, 184, 186; class size, 144; Free Academy, 177, 178; group intelligence tests, 99–100, 101; high school militancy, 161–162, 168; Junior High School Summer Program, 71; needle trades, 174; reading retardation, 22–23; social education program, 74; teacher training, 144–145; teacher transfers, 146; United Parent Association, 96
New York City Community College, 24
New York State Urban League, 121
New York Times, 14, 121
Noble, Gil, 121
noneducation, 22–25
Northside Center for Child Development, 30, 31
Notre Dame University, 176

Ocean Hill-Brownsville Demonstration District, 9, 128, 131; Bereiter-Engleman project, 11–13; and Board of Education, 115, 116, 119, 120; Governing Board, 114, 116–117, 129, 132; integration, 131–132; male volunteer teachers, 13–14; and news media, 121, 126; 1968 teacher strike, 126; origin of demonstration districts, 127; racism, 120, 121, 122; teacher aides, 11; transfer of 19 teachers, 120–122, 143; and UFT, 116, 117–122, 126, 129; unlicensed teachers, 127
Ohlin, Lloyd, 42
Oliver, C. Herbert, 111–132, 184; and JHS 271, 122
open admission, college, 4
Other America, 165

paraprofessionals, 10, 11, 16, 46, 186; Language Nurses, 71
parents: advisory committees, 92–93; apathetic, 106; associations of, 91, 96–97, 107; education of, 90–91; home visitation, 35–36, 93; and schools, 35–36, 89–90, 125; and teachers, 128–129

Parent-Teacher Association (PTA), 96, 97, 107
Passaic, delinquency study, 41–42
Peace Corps, 15
Perry School Project, Ypsilanti, 30
Philadelphia, 26, 133, 143
Pilgrim's Monument, Provincetown, 180
Plato, 111, 112
Politics, 111, 112
Polk, Kenneth, 41
Ponce de Leon, Juan, 152
Ponce, Puerto Rico, 155
poverty, and education, 64–65, 66
power structure, 47, 114
prediction, of delinquency, 59–62
preschool centers, 7, 8, 9, 10
printed media, in public relations, 93
private schools, class size, 10
professional accountability, 36–39, 123, 152, 154
professionalism, 13, 15, 16, 46, 133, 138–142, 143, 179–180
programmed instruction, 46
Project Headstart, 7, 25, 26, 30, 51; evaluation of, 69–70
promotion procedures, 136–137, 143
public relations, of schools: adult education, 91, 92; advisory committees, of parents, 92–93; concepts of, 82–84; conferences with parents, 89–90; definition, 81–82; and democracy, 85–86; home visitation, 93; in large urban districts, 87–88; levels of, 82; need for, 79–80; parent associations, 91; parent education, 90–91; parents, as resource visitors, 90; via personal contacts, 89; printed media, 93; recreational programs, 91, 92; techniques and media, 88–93
Puerto Ricans, 17, 20, 49, 104, 115, 118, 122, 131, 162; academic vs. general diplomas, 23–24, 149; bridge generation, 155, 158; college enrollment, 24; color problem, 158; commercial diplomas, 149; dropout rate, 23, 149; education vs. reality, 150, 153; and

English language, 152–153, 179; first generation, 154–155, 158; immigrants, in U.S., 150–152, 157–158; professional accountability, 152, 154; reading retardation, 22–23; second generation, 156–157; and slums, 151; and Spanish language, 151, 156–157
punitive-retaliatory orientation, of schools, 52
pupil evaluation, of teachers, 181–183
Pushkin, Alexander, 113, 121
Putnam, Paul, 161
Pygmalion in the Classroom, 30

Queens College, 24
Queens, New York, 14

racial issues, in high school militancy, 161, 170
racism, 120, 121, 122
Reader's Digest, 56
reading retardation, 22–23, 31; and delinquency, 59–60
Red Fights Back, 165
Reformation, 112
religion, in high school militancy, 162–163
Renaissance, 112
Republic, 111, 112
Richmond, Lynn, 41
Riis, Jacob, 20, 151
Rivlin, Harry N., 173–187
Robinson, Helen, 70
Robinson, Isaiah, 109
Rockefeller, Nelson A., 144
Rockland County, 145
Rockne, Knute, 176
Rousseau, J. J., 113
Russia, czarist, 113

Sahl, Mort, 3
St. Louis, 26
Salem, Massachusetts, 150
San Francisco, 9
San Juan, Puerto Rico, 155
Scandinavia, 177; day care centers, 7, 8, 9
Schapiro, Elliott, 95–110, 183

school-community relations, 75, 183–184; apathetic parents, 106; black community, 102, 103; black teachers, 104–105; and democratic society, 110; disruptive child, 104; employment without certification, 98; federal aid, 109–110; group intelligence tests, 99–100, 101; intelligence, and reading achievement, 99, 100; parent associations, 96–97, 107; passive, 98–99; teacher union, 102–103, 104, 105; teachers, and the poor, 102–103, 108, 110; and truth-telling, 107–108

School Improvement Program, Philadelphia, 26

School Segregation and Integration in the North, 21–22

schools, private, 6–7, 10

schools, public: age barriers, 50–51; authority structure, 47; black teachers, 127; clique-group structure, 49–50, communication lines, 48–49; and community agencies, 63; cultural-reconstruction mood, 53; cultural renewal, 56–58; delinquency, 41, 42, 44, 46, 50–54, 59–62, 63; dropout rate, 56, 66–67, 97–98; formal work structure, 46–47; Jewish dropout rate, 98; overt vs. subliminal curricula, 58–59; power structure, 47; punitive-retaliatory orientation, 52; special services, 62; status-prestige structure, 47–48; teacher's role, 54–56; therapeutic aid, for staff, 62–63; therapeutic mood, 53

school taxes, 130–131

Seale, Bobby, 164

second generation, Puerto Rican, 156–157

SEEK program, 76

segregation, 123–124

self-government, and the schools, 112–113, 122

Services for the Disruptive Child, 104, 105

Sexton, Pat, 146

Shanker, Albert, 120, 133–148, 187

Shaw, Bernard, 177

skills, mastery of, 68–70

snow patrol, 128–129

social education, 74

socioeconomic status (SES), 67

Southwestern Regional Educational Laboratory, 74

Spanish language, 151, 156–157

Sputnik, 80

states rights, 114

status-prestige structure, in schools, 47–48

Steffins, Lincoln, 151

Stokes, Carl, 164

street academies, 6

student power, 170

Students for a Democratic Society (SDS), 171

suspension, power of, 165–166

Supreme Court, U.S., 16, 21

teacher aides, 46, 70, 73

Teacher Retirement Board, 145

teachers: black, 127; competence of, 168–169; intra-system transfers, N.Y.C., 146; minority group, 17; and parents, 128–129, 130; and the poor, 102–103, 108, 110; rights of, 129–130; role of, 54–56; strikes, N.Y.C., 118, 126, 133, 164, 168; tenure laws, 169; training, 16–17, 144–145; turnover, 144–145; unlicensed, 127; young, 13–16

teacher unions, 10, 13, 102–103, 104, 105; bargaining rights, 133–134; civil rights, 133, 142–143; class size, 144; community control, 116, 125; economic benefits, 133–135, 143; effects of UFT salary contract, 145–146; grievance procedures, 137–138, 143; intra-system transfers, 146; professionalism, 133, 138–142, 143; promotion procedures, 136–137, 143; recency of, 134; snow patrol, 138–139; teacher strikes, 133, 164, 168; teacher training, 144–145; teacher turnover, 144–145; urban representation, 143–144

teaching aids, 17–18
teaching teams, 46
television, 18
therapeutic aid, for staff, 62–63
Third World, 5
Thorndike, E. L., 178
Title I, 25, 54, 71
Title III, 71
Todd, George, 121
Tolstoy, Leo, 123
Treaty of Guadalupe Hidalgo, 153

Union of Soviet Socialist Republics: educational system, 9–10; preschool care centers, 7–8, 9; Schools of the Extended Day, 8; Sputnik, 80; urbanization problems, 9–10
United Federation of Teacher, 38, 104, 125, 133, 144; N.Y.C. salary contract, 145–146; and Ocean Hill-Brownsville district, 116, 117–122, 126, 129; teacher strike, 1967, 118
United Parent Association, N.Y.C., 96
United States Office of Education, 54, 58, 161
universal national service, 15–16
University of Texas, 74
Upward Bound program, 25, 26, 31, 71, 76
urban decay, 3–4, 5
Urban Grants Act, 109

Urban League Street Academy, 174
Urban Research Corporation, 161

Vairo, Philip D., 160–172, 183, 187
Vann, Albert, 164
Vietnam war, 13
violence, student, 169
vocational diploma, 166

Wallace, George, 114
Wally, James, 140, 141
Washington, D.C., 133, 143
Weinstein, Gerald, 34
welfare dependency, 65–66
Westchester County, 145; OEO program, 76
Westminster Bethany United Presbyterian Church, 116
West Virginia, 75
White Faces, Black Masks, 165
Whitman, Walt, 152
Wilkerson, Doxey A., 19–39
Wilson, Charles, 164
WINS Radio, 121
WLIB Radio, 121
WNEW Radio, 121
Work Project Administration, 110
work structure, in schools, 46–47
Wretched of the Earth, 165
Wright, Samuel, 124
WWRL Radio, 121

Ypsilanti, 30